Freudenberg Family Genealogy

Larry Walter Freudenberg

Freudenberg Family Genealogy

Larry Walter Freudenberg

Freudenberg Family Genealogy
by Larry Walter Freudenberg

Printed in the United States of America

TSA Publications
1052 Gardner Road
Charleston, SC 29407
www.larryfreudenberg.com
Interior Design by Larry Freudenberg

This Volume is dedicated to my parents who are dedicated to living a life as American Jews and to this country for welcoming my father, grandmother and grandfather in 1940 when doors were closed everywhere for Jews seeking asylum.

Table of Contents

Generation No. 1

1. Cara Michelle Freudenberg, born August 08, 1984 in Atlanta, Georgia. She was the daughter of **2. Larry Walter Freudenberg** and **3. Marsha Ruth Jacobs.**

More About Cara Michelle Freudenberg:
Bat Mitzvah: 1996, Jerusalem, Israel at the Southern Wall of the Kotel
Elementary School: Addlestone Hebrew Academy, Charleston, SC
Hebrew Name: Catrella Bat Miriam
High School: Bishop England High School, Daniel Island, SC
College: 2007 Graduate, UGA. Postgraduate: Argosy University, Atlanta earning Psy.D.
Hospital of birth: August 08, 1984, Born at Northside Hospital. C Section birth.

1. Stephen Triest Freudenberg, born November 06, 1989 in Charleston, South Carolina. He was the son of **2. Larry Walter Freudenberg** and **3. Marsha Ruth Jacobs.**

More About Stephen Triest Freudenberg:
Bar Mitzvah: November 16, 2002, Brith Sholom Beth Israel, Charleston, SC
Bris Milah: November 13, 1989, Brit Milah at his home on 1901 Sandcroft Drive. Rabbi Edward Friedman
Elementary School: Addlestone Hebrew Academy, Charleston, SC
Hebrew Name: Simcha Ben Eliyahu

1

High School: Academic Magnet HS - 9th and 10th grade. Porter-Gaud HS - 11th and 12th grades.
Hospital of birth: November 06, 1989, Born at Roper Hospital

Generation No. 2

2. Larry Walter Freudenberg, born April 13, 1959 in Charleston, South Carolina. He was the son of **4. Colonel (US Army Reserve) Henry Heineman Freudenberg** and **5. Maxine Anne Triest.** He married **3. Marsha Ruth Jacobs** September 06, 1981 in Atlanta, Georgia.

3. Marsha Ruth Jacobs, born October 29, 1958 in Atlanta, Georgia. She was the daughter of **6. Harris Jacobs** and **7. Katherine Rae Stock.**

Notes for Larry Walter Freudenberg:
Published two "Source" books for the Charleston Jewish Community Center 1993 and 1995. Copies in LWF archives.
1994 received member of the year from the Charleston Jewish Community Center
1996 Board of Addlestone Hebrew Academy
December 1994. Recited my first Haftorah. Varikra at Brith Shalom Beth Israel Synagogue in Charleston, SC in honor of the memory of my late father in law, Harris Jacobs on his first yahrzeit. I was tutored by Rabbi Avram Bogopulsky.
November 11, 1995. Recited my second Haftorah. Variki at Brith Sholom Beth Israel Synagogue in Charleston, SC in honor of my wife's birthday. Tutored by Rabbi Bogopulsky.
National Honor Society in High School.

More About Larry Walter Freudenberg:
Bar Mitzvah: April 1971, Bar Mitzvah at KKBE in Charleston, SC
Clubs: 1983, Founder and President Sidney Marcus B'nai B'rith, Atlanta
Elementary School: Attended Orange Grove Elementary School 1st - 5th grade
Employment: June 1981, First job as college grad. Management Associate with National Bank of Georgia
Hebrew Name: Eliyahu Ben Zve
High School: May 30, 1977, Attended College Preparatory School on Archdale Street. 7th -12 Grade.
Hospital of birth: April 13, 1959, Born at Roper Hospital
Middle School: Attended Wallace Middle School 6th Grade
Occupation: June 01, 1981 - May 01, 1986, Assistant Vice President National Bank of Georgia
Profession: June 11, 1994, Presented Certified Insurance Counselor (CIC)
Undergraduate: 1981, Graduated BBA in Marketing from University of Georgia, Athens, GA

Below is a copy of an interview with Moment Magazine (www.momentmag.com) Founded by Elie Wiesel and Leonard Fein, first hit newsstands in May 1975. The magazine was doing a story on the exhibit about Jews of South Carolina which just opened in Columbia, South Carolina and will travel around the country.

Dear Mr. Freudenberg,

3

I was given your name by Dale Rosengarten, curator of the exhibit, "A Portion of the People," about the Jews of South Carolina. My name is Nathan Kleinman, I'm a student at Georgetown and Editorial Intern at Moment Magazine, a bimonthly magazine of Jewish culture, politics, and religion. I'm writing an article on that exhibit, and Dale told me that you could be a good source. I would love to ask you some questions if you have the time. I can do it over email, if that's easiest, or over the phone, if you'd prefer. I would particularly like to hear about what you lent to the show. Thank you very much for your time.
Sincerely,
Nathan Kleinman

1. When did your family settle in South Carolina? How did they find there way there, and, if you have any idea, what led them to choose South Carolina? My great-grandfather's grandfather, Joseph Triest (born 1810) and his son, Maier Triest (born 1831), my great great grandfather came to America from the Kingdom of Bavaria in 1850. I don't know why they settled in Charleston. Just lucky, I guess!

2. What do you think it was like for the early members of your family as Jews in South Carolina? I am sure it was better than living in Europe at that time but no sooner than they got settled, the war of northern aggression started in 1860 at Fort Sumter in Charleston. Information about Maier Triest from Historian, Robert Rosen. 10/23/97. Given to me by Robert from his research on my great great grandfather for his book **The Jewish Confederates** by Robert Rosen, published in Columbia, SC by the University of SC Press. Maier Triest, whose family had come

4

from Bavaria in the early part of the 19th century, was born in 1831. He was thirty years old when the war (Civil War) started and served as Captain of Triest's Col. (Beat 2), 16th SC Militia from November 9 to December 20, 1861. As most young, able-bodied Charlestonians served in a militia unit prior to the war, Triest undoubtedly served in one such organization as this company bears his name, and he served as Captain. In January, 1862, Triest and hundreds of other South Carolinians enlisted in the 24th SC Volunteers, a regiment raised by Colonel Clement H. Steven, who had formerly commanded Triest's militia regiment and may have known Triest prior to that time. The 24th was originally organized by Stevens and Lt. Colonel Ellison Capers for twelve months of Confederate service. Six companies were raised for one year when state policy changed in March, 1862, to require service for the duration of the war. All the men agreed to so serve. (Rivers Account of the Raising of Troops in South Carolina for State and Confederate Service 1861 - 1865, Columbia, SC, The Bryan Publishing Company, 1899, pages 29-30,) Colonel Stevens chose Triest to be Sergeant-Major of the 24th SC, whereupon Triest re-enlisted at that rank on January 20, 1862 (C.S.R.). In January, 1863, he was promoted to Regimental Quartermaster Sergeant, a position he held throughout the war. Rabbi Elzas (who, of course, knew Triest and his family) wrote that Triest was "promoted twice to A.A.A. General, once by General Stevens, who died before commission was returned, and again by General Capers just before the close of the war." (page. 235) [The compiled service records neither corroborate nor contradict this statement]. The 24th saw action

5

throughout the war at Secessionville (SC), Jackson, Mississippi (Vicksburg campaign), Atlanta, Franklin, Nashville and the Carolinas. Triest was with the 24th in the weeks before the final assault on Vicksburg, when Grant attempted to get between Vicksburg, the Confederate stronghold on the Mississippi River, and the Confederate forces at Jackson, a city and rail hub --- miles to the east of Vicksburg. The South Carolinians were determined to prevent Jackson from falling to Grant's army. The 24th was engaged in fierce, hand-to-hand combat with the 10th Missouri. At Wright's Farm, a ball hit Colonel Ellison Caper's horse and a number of men of the 24th were killed. Capers wrote afterwards that Triest had given him "a most welcomed drink of whiskey." It was the only time Capers said he ever took a drink during the war. (Enlisted for the War, The Struggles of the Gallant 24th Regiment, South Carolina Volunteers, 1861 - 1865), Eugene W. Jones, Jr. , Longstreet House, Hightown, NJ, 1997; on Triest, see pages 15, 91, 214; Capers letter dated May 17, 1863, South Carolina Library, USC). As Regimental Quartermaster Sergeant, it was Triest's job to see to it that the entire regiment was supplied. During the Jackson campaign, for example, he traveled to Canton and Meridian, Mississippi, to obtain shoes and clothing which had been left behind in storage at the beginning of the campaign. He traveled throughout July and August, 1863, retrieving and transporting boxes of clothing, cooking utensils and supplies. In early October, 1863, while at Chickamauga, Tenn., Triest was sent to Columbia and Charleston by General Braxton Bragg to act as agent for the collection of winter clothes, blankets and other supplies from the SC Relief Association. He returned on October 28 having used his own funds for "drayage" (movement by wagon) and cooperage (crating) at stops along the way. (The funds were refunded to him.) He surrendered with the consolidated and redesignated 16th/24th SC Regiment with General Joseph E. Johnston's Army on April 26, 1865. He was paroled on May 1. According to Elzas, Triest was wounded at Atlanta (235). Reprinted by permission from Robert Rosen. Compiled by Rosen for a presentation to the Sisterhood at Kahal Kadosh Beth Elohim, October. 25, 1997.

3. How do you think your experience as a Jew in South Carolina has been different from, say, the experience of a Jew growing up in Philadelphia, or Brooklyn? (if you think it has been different). I guess like most Jews in America, I am a mixed bag. From my mother's family, the Triest's, I am the 6th generation in America and in South Carolina. All of the 3rd generation Triest family (after Joseph & Maier) except my great grandfather, Montague moved to New York. My grandfather, Maier, who was named after his grandfather, was the proudest Charlestonian you would have ever met. He was active in B'nai B'rith and started the first AZA chapter in Charleston. But he was born in NYC. His mother was visiting family in NYC when she went into labor. My great grandfather, Montague and grandfather, Maier attended Columbia. I am also a 11th generation American on my mother's maternal side of the family. One of the oldest Jewish family lines in America dating to the 1696. Abraham Isaacs is buried in NYC.

My father is a Holocaust survivor. Mixed bag! I cannot compare my life to NYC or Phil because I grew up in Charleston and went to college in Georgia at the University of Ga. I lived in Atlanta for a few years but never a "northern" city. In grade school I remember always being either the only Jew or one of only a few. I never hid my Judaism and tried to educate my friends and classmates about Judaism. You really become proud of your Judaism when you live in a city like Charleston. SC has been very good the the Jews. We were allowed to worship freely and openly as Jews from colonial times.

4. What did you lend to the exhibit, and what is important about that piece (or those pieces) in terms of your family history? Also, what lessons do you think Jews throughout America and the world can learn from "A Portion of the People"? Our family loaned a few items:

- Our family Bible of Montague Triest. It includes a basic family tree.
- My grandfather's toys. We have several antique metal toys of Maier Triest. They're from the turn of the 20th century.
- A portrait (original painting) of my great great grandmother Rebecca Elias Israel (B.: 1839 d: 1896). Buried in the historic Coming Street Cemetery in Charleston.
- Misc. photos of my family from the early 20th century.

All of the items are extremely valuable to me because they're links to my heritage in SC. The toys are not Judaic. The photos don't show Jews with kippas. The portrait shows a dignified "southern" lady with her beautiful jewelry. They blended into the community but I am so proud that they didn't just maintain their

Judaism for many generations, they were "serious" Jews. They were leaders in Jewish organizations like B'nai B'rith, Kahal Kadosh Beth Elohim Temple (5 members of my family have been Presidents). My mother, Maxine Triest Freudenberg is the current President of the congregation.); Hebrew Orphans Society, Hebrew Benevolent Society. Non-Jewish organizations like Elks, Sertoma, American Cancer Society... Montague(great-grandfather) and Maier Triest (grandfather) were Chairman of the Charleston School Board. My children, Cara Michelle Freudenberg (17) and Stephen Triest Freudenberg (12) are 7th generation SC Jews! And G-d willing, they'll have another 7 generation following them that maintain their Jewish roots in SC!

5. What lesson can people learn from the exhibit? I think Jews from places other than southern towns and cities will be amazed. I hate to generalize but most Jews from the north and the west, have absolutely no idea that Jews live in places like SC! They don't know that Charleston once had the largest Jewish population in America. This is not amazing information for me. I love being a Jewish South Carolinian and cannot imagine being Jewish anywhere else. Our history has been ignored by the Jewish historians of this country as if we didn't exist. When in realty, it all started here! Established in 1749, Congregation Kahal Kadosh Beth Elohim in Charleston, SC became the first Reform Jewish congregation in the United States in 1841. The Coming Street Cemetery in Charleston where most of my family is buried is one of the oldest Jewish burial grounds in the United States dating back to the Colonial period. We have the oldest Orthodox congregation in the south, Brith

9

Sholom Beth Israel(founded 1854). We have the oldest Jewish charitable society in America, The Hebrew Benevolent Society founded in 1784. Hebrew Orphans Society, founded 1801 is the oldest incorporated Jewish charitable society in America. The exhibit is priceless. It paints a picture of the Jews of SC. Dale Rosengarten from the College of Charleston has done a magnificent job. She has done a brilliant job. Nathan, email if you need anything else. I hope this helps.

More About Marsha Ruth Jacobs:
Elementary School: Kittridge in Atlanta
Hebrew Name: Miriam
High School: May 30, 1976, Briarcliff High in Atlanta.
Hospital of birth: October 29, 1958, Georgia Baptist in Atlanta
Masters Degree: Masters Degree in Education. -Georgia State University
Occupation: Teacher
Undergraduate: May 1981, BBS in Education from the University of Ga.
Awards: Named Addlestone Teacher of the Year and Best Pre-school Teacher in Charleston by the readers of Parent's Magazine.

Marriage Notes for Larry Freudenberg and Marsha Jacobs:
Married by Rabbi Harry Epstein and Cantor Goodfriend at Ahavath Achim Congregation in Atlanta. Rabbi Epstein married Marsha's parents. The Ketubah was witnessed by Alan Silverman (friend) and Loran Greenstein (Husband of Marsha's 1st Cousin Jackie Stein Greenstein). Marsha's father Harris Jacobs gave her away. Marsha and Larry honeymooned on a Holland America Cruise

(Veendam) from NYC to Bermuda in 1982.

Children of Larry Freudenberg and Marsha Jacobs are:

    i. Cara Michelle Freudenberg, born August 08, 1984 in Atlanta, Georgia.

    ii. Stephen Triest Freudenberg, born November 06, 1989 in Charleston, South Carolina.

Generation No. 3

    4. Henry Heineman Freudenberg, born April 02, 1929 in Essen, Germany. He was the son of **8. Walter Freudenberg** and **9. Margot Strauss**. He married **5. Maxine Anne Triest** January 07, 1951 in Charleston, South Carolina.

    5. Maxine Anne Triest, born September 14, 1930 in Charleston, South Carolina. She was the daughter of **10. Maier Triest** and **11. Miriam Hendricks Neuberger.**

Notes for Henry Heineman Freudenberg:
Biography prepared by Henry H. Freudenberg
Colonel, Army of the United States (Retired)
Born: April 2, 1929, Essen Germany. Immigrated to the US with parents in 1940 after spending 1 year in Great Britain. Son of Walter Freudenberg (deceased 12/31/1952 in Charleston) and Margot Strauss Freudenberg, R.P.T.; DHL (Honorary. MUSC)
Education: Elementary grades in Germany and London 1939-1940
Charleston, SC Public Schools, High School of Charleston, 1946, The Citadel, BA Pol. SC. 1950
Military: Commissioned 2d Lieutenant Army of the

11

United States 1950

Service: Served on Active Duty and Reserve until October 1982

Served as an Ordnance Ammunition Officer in Korea 1951-1952.

Staff and Command Assignments until retirement at the rank of Colonel.

American Defense Medal, United Nations Award, Korean

Decorations: Service Medal, Army Reserve Medal with 3 clusters, Meritorious Service Medal with 3 Oak Leaf Clusters.

Civilian: President & CEO Triest & Sholk Inc. 1953-1995

Occupation: Independent Insurance Agency founded in 1903

Civic, social and religious: Sertoma Club of Charleston: Charter member, Life Member and Past President.

Charleston Metro Chamber of Commerce: Offices and positions held; Vice President of Travel, Tourism and Conventions Division, Chairman Of the Red Carpet Club; The Small Business Council; The West Ashley Area Council and Chair of the Accreditation Committee.

Family Services, Inc. Board member 1963 through December 21, 1999 when I was appointed as Chairman Emeritus.

Offices held: Secretary, Vice President, and President/Chairman 1967-1968, 1991-1992 and 1995.

The Hebrew Benevolent Society founded 1784: Member since 1954, Trustee for some 25+ years, Past Secretary & Treasurer, 2 terms and President for 2 terms.

The Hebrew Orphan Society of Charleston SC

founded on July 15, 1801 and Incorporated on that date by the Legislature of SC. The

Membership is limited to 36 individuals, male and female.

Member since October 29, 1975, Secretary & Treasurer 1988-2000,

Vice President 2001 and President 2002.

The N. Edgar Miles, MD Scholarship Fund of the Hebrew Orphan Society, since 1994 which provides College Scholarships to SC High School graduates, based on financial need and academic excellence, irrespective of race or religion.

I have been the Fund Secretary and manager since its inception in 1994.

Charleston Jewish Community Center and Charleston Jewish Community Services: Member for over 25 years.

Kahal Kadosh Beth Elohim Synagogue: Member since 1940 arrival in Charleston. Offices Held: President of the Men's Club in 1957; Trustee, Secretary, Vice President and President of the Synagogue 1969-1971. Vice President of Finance 1995-1996.

Founder and President of the Congregation Kahal Kadosh Beth Elohim Endowment Fund, Inc. since it's founding in 1995.

Vice Chairman of the 5 Million Dollar Capital Campaign 1998-2000.

Charleston Post & Courier High Profile Article published - Saturday, April 17, 2004
By Jennifer Hawes Berry, Of **The Post and Courier** Staff

Henry Freudenberg

13

Business Leader Finds Rebirth
and Community to Serve

"His German passport shows a boy of 10 with sweet eyes and no smile. Stamped on it are swastikas and the middle name forced on him by the Nazis: Israel. It seems so long ago. Henry H. Freudenberg has just turned 75, so many lifetimes from the days when his future almost wasn't. But don't expect him to tell an old man's story. Freudenberg sits in his office at a flat-screen computer one recent morning scanning a picture of flames on CO-OWN's Web site for news on Iraq and Israel. He checks his calendar. Checks his e-mail. Henry H. Freudenberg came to Charleston as a boy of 10 after his family fled Nazi Germany. He built a life here as an Army man, husband, father and businessman. For all that, he considers himself one of the luckiest men alive on the eve of this year's Holocaust Remembrance Day. "Damn computers," he grins, trying to act the grumpy old man he's not. cell phone chimes out a song. It's his mother, Margot, who needs to reschedule their weekly lunch. He pulls out his Palm V and starts poking in the change. He and his wife, Maxine, have matching ones so they can download them to their home computer. "He likes his gadgets," jokes his son, Larry, who now runs the family business. Freudenberg turns back to the CNN Web page full of stories about Iraq and terrorist killings. Talk quickly turns to Iraq and the way hatred can spread across the world. Freudenberg closely follows the news from the Middle East. It brings back memories he prefers to forget. Sunday is Holocaust Remembrance Day, but Freudenberg has no special plans. He doesn't consider himself a survivor. Just mention the Holocaust, about those who escaped the massive death, and Freudenberg leans forward in his chair. He takes off his glasses and sets them aside, his sky-blue eyes turning intense. His words are tinged by a mix of German and Broad Street Charleston. So listen closely.

14

"I feel we are the luckiest people in the world. We got out before the war started, before the Nazis rounded people up, put them into cable cars and sent them to concentration camps," he says. "I grieve for Holocaust survivors. But I'm not one of them." He points to local survivors who barely escaped the death camps. His parents suffered. But not he, though he was there, as the boy in the passport photo.

ARRIVAL OF HITLER

As a child, Freudenberg needed surgery for a neck problem. It was 1938, and already doctors wouldn't touch a Jewish child. His mother found a nun who ran a tiny hospital and knew a doctor just back from America who would do it. Then came an order that no Jew was to be in the streets. After the operation, the doctor called to say that a Nazi nurse had reported the nun for harboring a Jewish child. Mrs. Freudenberg went to get her son. She found him in a cast from head to groin. She sneaked him home and put him to bed. Six weeks later, she cut off the cast with scissors the doctor had given her. The boy's neck wasn't straight. She found the doctor again. He met them in a church basement at midnight and put on another cast. This time it worked. At the same time, she had to protect her husband, Walter, who had become involved in activities that he later realized opposed the Nazis. Four times she hid him from the Nazis. Then one night when they went to synagogue, despite the orders not to, their rabbi warned: "It might be that we do not see each other anymore." The next day, nine others who'd come to synagogue just the day before committed suicide. Mrs. Freudenberg left her synagogue in flames. Soon after, she found herself being interrogated by the Gestapo. She was released, and the Nazis never found her husband. There was a quota system for those who wanted to leave. Their number came up quickly. Of all this, Henry Freudenberg recalls little, wants to recall

15

little all these years later. Where his mother still hears the Nazi soldiers marching through her hometown and can see the truckloads of Jews being taken away for their own "protection" to concentration camps, Freudenberg recalls nothing. About the huge department store in Essen his family ran that wrapped around a main intersection, Freudenberg recalls nothing. Instead, he has much different memories, ones about a life's rebirth in Charleston. That journey began when his family boarded a steamer with round-trip tickets to England. "Ostensibly to go on vacation," he recalls, "without any intention of returning." Mr. Freudenberg left wearing the medals he'd earned fighting for Germany on two fronts in World War I, including his Iron Cross. A few months later, Germany invaded Poland and started World War II.

ARRIVING IN HEAVEN

They stayed in England for a year. They became stateless when Germany revoked their citizenship, even asked his father to return his Iron Cross. There Freudenberg's memories pick up. He recalls going to school in London until the British feared Hitler would bomb the city. The students moved to the country. In 1940, the Freudenbergs learned they could come to America. They landed in New York, and a family member in Greenville suggested Charleston. The family boarded a plane in frigid New York and landed in a Charleston sauna. They arrived with $2.50. They went to Congregation Beth Elohim, the city's Reform temple. They had no money, few possessions, nothing really. The local Jewish community took them in. One man guaranteed their rent. A woman opened doors for them. His mother set up a physical therapy practice back in a day when very few women ran their own businesses. The daughter of a prominent pediatrician, Mrs. Freudenberg would become a Charleston icon for her community service. The family rented an apartment downtown where Freudenberg found a world where

16

people left the doors unlocked. People were friendly, and he quickly made friends at Beth Elohim. "I felt like I was in heaven," he recalls. "You could go where you wanted, do what you wanted." Among the families who welcomed them when they arrived were the Triests. Maier Triest invited them over for dinner one night. When the Freudenbergs arrived, Triest's daughter, Maxine Anne, was upstairs. Her mom hollered, "Come on down, there's a cute boy down here!" Freudenberg was 11, Maxine 9 or 10. They would become friends. Somewhere along the line, around when Freudenberg was 14, they began to date -- or as close to dating as kids back then did at that age. They'd go together, split up, go together again. They were young.

PAYING DEBTS

Freudenberg entered The Citadel in 1946, a day high with patriotic fervor. He agreed to an Army commission after he graduated in 1950. "I had a debt to pay this country for the opportunities afforded me," he says. He enlisted as a second lieutenant in the Army and was assigned to the Korean War. By then, he and Maxine had married. And Maxine was pregnant. Freudenberg asked his colonel for a few months deferment before shipping out so he could be home when his first baby was born. The answer: No. So he went. Maxine stayed in Charleston with her parents. He was a depot officer for an ordnance and ammunition depot. They received and reissued ordnance "and tried not to get blown up." Once he was shot at, though the bullet took out only the windshield of his vehicle. Another time, a man sitting beside him was shot and killed. Freudenberg shies away from talking much about those days. "At 21, you're invincible," he says. "Besides, I was not a foot soldier. And I refused to jump out of a perfectly good airplane." While in Korea, he also got a call from the Red Cross. "Hey lieutenant! Congratulations, you're a daddy!" He'd spent

17

nearly five months in Korea when his father became gravely ill.
Freudenberg returned home, and his father died December. 31,
1952. Walter Freudenberg wasn't a demonstrative father, but
he set an example of decency. He never gave the Germans back
his Iron Cross, not after fighting on two fronts and against the
communists on behalf of a country that would have killed him.
And he got his family to a place where his only child could live
a dream, not a nightmare.

FAMILY BUSINESS

Freudenberg had married Maxine in 1951. When he returned
home from Korea to the arms of his wife and newborn son, his
father-in-law posed a question: "Do you want to stay in the
Army? Or do you want to work for a living?" Maier Triest
offered Freudenberg $75 a week to work as an insurance agent
at his firm, Triest & Sholk Agency. Freudenberg chose both.
He went to work for the insurance agency founded in 1903 by
Maxine's grandfather, Montague Triest, on Broad Street. He
would stay for 51 years. He started as an insurance agent and
worked his way up to president in 1970. Meanwhile, he and
Maxine raised two daughters and a son. Freudenberg also
worked with the Army Reserve until he retired in 1982 at the
rank of colonel. Meanwhile, his son, Larry, grew up, became a
banker and moved to Atlanta. Then Freudenberg neared
retirement age and thought of selling the business that had
remained in their family since its birth in 1903. Larry moved
home shortly before Hurricane Hugo hit. He had tired of the
corporate life and wanted to return to Charleston. In 1996,
Freudenberg handed the insurance agency over to Larry,
keeping it in the family for another generation.

JOINING IN

Like his mother, Freudenberg is what you'd call a "joiner."

18

He's been an Elk, a Mason, cofounder and president of the Sertoma Club of Charleston and president of Family Service of Charleston County (a United Way agency), to name a few. In 1967, he was named president of the Hebrew Benevolent Society. He's also been president of its sister society, the Hebrew Orphan Society. But perhaps his greatest passion -- and that of Maxine's -- has been their temple. Freudenberg served as president of Beth Elohim, the oldest surviving Reform temple in the world. He jokes that the temple had only 150 families, "so they were desperate" for someone to take the position. In truth, he'd married into a family active at Beth Elohim. Maxine was born into the temple and is the immediate past president. She'd had family members serve as president. Her grandmother was a daily presence. Her family, including Freudenberg, donated a Torah scroll used in worship. "He's certainly been a very active leader for many decades," Rabbi Anthony Holz says. "He cares very deeply about the temple, about the congregation and has shown it in a number of ways over the years." A few years ago, good friend Dr. Gordon Stine nominated Freudenberg for the state's highest award for community service. In 2002, Gov. Jim Hodges awarded him The Order of the Silver Crescent. It was Stine who installed Freudenberg as president of the temple. Today, he recalls the 40 years they've collaborated on projects, from creating scholarships to honoring Beth Elohim's 250th anniversary. "You can never do anything if you don't have a good team. You can't do it yourself," Stine says. "He's always willing to go along with you and help you."

NO SURVIVOR

Larry Freudenberg tells of visiting a Holocaust museum in Israel. The museum was gathering profiles of the 6 million Jews killed. One profile caught his eye. It was a German passport, one with a young boy who looked so much like his father back in 1939, the year the Freudenbergs were able to leave

19

Germany. This boy, however, died in a concentration camp. "There but for the grace of God ... ," Larry ponders. Freudenberg hasn't returned to Germany since that day in 1939. Doesn't want to. He still worries about what he'd find there, or what might find him. America is, has been, his home. "I seriously doubt we would have had the opportunities, even under a non-Hitler government, that we had here," Freudenberg says. "America really is the land of opportunity -- if you're willing to work for it."

Henry Freudenberg
AGE: 75

FAMILY: Wife Maxine Anne; son, Larry; and daughters, Lynn Plait and Nancy Cherson. Five grandchildren.

WHY DID YOU ATTEND THE CITADEL? "Because my mother said I would!" He graduated from the Corps of Cadets in 1950.

MILITARY EDUCATION: The Ordnance School, Aberdeen Proving Grounds; The Transportation Officers School; Command and General Staff College; and the Industrial College of the Armed Forces in Washington, D.C.

COMMUNITY WORK: Chairman emeritus of Family Services Inc., past president of Congregation Beth Elohim, past president of Sertoma Club of Charleston, various positions with the Charleston Metro Chamber of Commerce, past president of Hebrew Benevolent Society, past president of Hebrew Orphan Society of Charleston, and 25-year member of Charleston Jewish Community Center and Charleston Jewish Community Services.

AWARDS: In 2002, Gov. Jim Hodges awarded him The

20

Order of the Silver Crescent, the state's highest honor for civic service. Military awards include the American Defense Medal, United Nations Award, Korean Service Medal, Army Reserve Medal with three clusters and Meritorious Service Medal with three Oak Leaf Clusters.

SYNAGOGUE AFFILIATION: Congregation Beth Elohim, which he's attended since arriving in Charleston in 1940.

WHAT ARE YOUR HOBBIES? "I've got a nice boat that I haven't gotten out on. The weather's been lousy!"

WHAT ARE YOU READING TODAY? Suspense thriller "The Da Vinci Code" by Dan Brown. "I just started it, but I keep falling asleep."

MOMENT OF FAME: In 1969, he was on an airplane *flight home to Charleston when the pilot announced they were diverting to Utah "because of a terrible weather front." They circled for some time before the doctor beside him noticed, "Hey guys, I see palm trees!" The pilot returned to say, "Welcome to Cuba." Turned out, they'd been hijacked. Cuban soldiers came aboard and got the hijacker. Freudenberg saw them leading the man away with rifles. They spent a few hours in Cuba enjoying food, cigars and propaganda before heading home."*

More About Colonel (USA) Henry Heineman Freudenberg:
Bar Mitzvah: Kahal Kadosh Beth Elohim
Clubs: President, Charleston Sertoma
Elementary School: Craft School, Charleston, SC
Hebrew Name: Zvie ben Walter
High School: Charleston High
Military service: Colonel, US Army - Served in Korea
Synagogue: Kahal Kadosh Beth Elohim

Undergraduate: 1950, The Citadel, Charleston, SC

More About Maxine Anne Triest:
High School: Ashley Hall, Charleston, SC
Hospital of birth: Roper, Charleston, SC
Synagogue: Kahal Kadosh Beth Elohim
Undergraduate: University of Georgia, Athens, Georgia

More About Henry Freudenberg and Maxine Triest:
Marriage:
January 07, 1951, Charleston, South Carolina
Marriage date: Married in Kahal Kadosh Beth Elohim Temple by Rabbi Alan Tarsish

Children of Henry Freudenberg and Maxine Triest are:
      i.   Lynn Freudenberg, born April 20, 1952 in Charleston, South Carolina; married Sidney Ross Plait August 29, 1982 in Atlanta, Georgia; born December 06, 1954 in Chicago, Illinois.

Notes for Lynn Freudenberg:
Lynn Freudenberg Plait (Written by Lynn F. Plait. 12/11/00.
Graduated St. Andrews High School, Charleston, SC, June 1970.
Graduated University of Florida, Gainesville, FL, March 1974, BA Sociology with Honors.
Graduated Atlanta University, Atlanta, GA, May 1976, Masters in Social Work with Concentration in Policy and Planning.
First career as Program Specialist at Senior Citizen Services of Metro Atlanta, 1976 - 1979.
Second career began as an Employee Relations

Specialist at The First National Bank of Atlanta, 1979 - 1982.

Married Sid Plait on August 29, 1982, at the Tower Place Hotel, Atlanta, GA. Wedding ceremony performed by both Rabbi Donald Tam from Temple Emanu-El in Atlanta and Rabbi Itzak Klirs of Congregation Olam Tikvah in Fairfield, VA. Sid was Rabbi Klir's first Bar Mitzvah upon his becoming rabbi at the congregation in VA. The couple honeymooned in Banff and Victoria in Western Canada and Seattle, WA. They settled into their first home in Decatur, GA. Lynn's husband Sid graduated from the Georgia Institute of Technology in 1978 with a Bachelors Degree in Computer Science. Sid is the oldest son of Evelyn and Alan Plait of Sarasota, FL and formerly of Springfield, VA. He has three younger siblings, Merril, Marcia, and Philip. Immediately upon return from the honeymoon, Lynn joined the Management Associate Program at First Atlanta and began the remainder of her 21 year career at First Atlanta (to later merge and become Wachovia Bank). She attained a rank of Vice President and ended her career there in August 2000 after serving the last ten years in the Private Banking Division.

During this time, Lynn and Sid became the parents of Lindsey Erin Plait (born July 5, 1984). Lindsey attended The Children's School in Atlanta, GA, from 1987 until 1996 when she graduated at the end of the sixth grade. She then attended public schools in North Fulton County, GA. She will graduate from Centennial High School in June 2002.

More About Sidney Plait and Lynn Freudenberg:
Marriage: August 29, 1982, Atlanta, Georgia

ii. Nancy Freudenberg, born September 02, 1955 in Charleston, South Carolina; married Brad Michael Cherson February 15, 1981 in Charleston, South Carolina; born September 02, 1957 in High Point, North Carolina.

More About Nancy Freudenberg:
Graduate: Middleton High School, Charleston, SC
Graduate: University of Maryland
Graduate: December 1979, Pediatric Physicians Assistant. Medical University of SC

More About Brad Cherson and Nancy Freudenberg:
Marriage: February 15, 1981, Charleston, South Carolina. Kahal Kadosh Beth Elohim. Rabbi William Rosenthal

iii. Larry Walter Freudenberg, born April 13, 1959 in Charleston, South Carolina; married Marsha Ruth Jacobs September 06, 1981 in Atlanta, Georgia.

6. Harris Jacobs, born May 21, 1930 in Atlanta, Georgia; died December 22, 1993 in Atlanta, Georgia. He was the son of **12. Joseph Jacobs** and **13. Esther Rosenwald.** He married **7. Katherine Rae Stock** December 27 in Rome, Georgia.
7. Katherine Rae Stock, born June 21, 1931 in Rome, Georgia. She was the daughter of **14. Casper Isadore Stock** and **15. Sarah Francis Esserman.**

Notes for Harris Jacobs:
Excerpt of speech honoring Harris with the Lodge's award for exceptional service to the community.
"Honored Rabbis, Friends, and Guests of B'nai B'rith
One of the highlights of this eventful evening is the presentation

of the Gate City Lodge B'nai B'rith Distinguished Service Award to Harris Jacobs. It is the most coveted award in the Jewish Community. Why this particular man? Distinguished he is... Where did his record of distinguished services begin? What are the unique qualities of his services? Our honoree is known for his tremendous compassion, stamina, and desire to be involved. This desire could have been one for personal success — which he certainly has attained. Fortunately, for our entire community, it has been more than that. Harris Jacobs has been involved in making Atlanta a better place to live. He is a man of responsibility. On Kol Nidre night in September of 1966, Rabbi Harry Epstein's "sermon was on the word "responsibility". He said that it is the most important word in the English language. I would like to quote a very meaningful and memorable paragraph from his sermon. Rabbi Epstein said, and I quote ..." A totally uninvolved person is 'out of this world". One must be related to others; and to feel oneself joined to others is to feel oneself responsible. So, then, responsibility is not as we think, something thrust upon us from without. It is rather the very condition of being fully human. To be human means to practice self-discipline because of our concern and love for causes and people with whom we identify". This exemplifies Harris Jacobs. He is fully human. He has concern and love for people and for causes with which he identifies. Harris Jacobs' keen sense of responsibility and his desire for involvement is coupled with intelligence and extraordinary ability. A city is fortunate when such a man's satisfaction lies beyond his personal fulfillment. Then we have the makings of a man who contributes in full measure to the well-being of his community. Then we have a man worthy of our Gate City Lodge Distinguished Service Award."

More About Harris Jacobs:
Cause of Death: cardiac arrest at age 63
Hebrew Name: Hershel Ben Yosef Halevi

Medical Information: Heart attack at age 50.
Lover of athletics
Beloved Community leader and Philanthropist in
Atlanta, Georgia
National leader in Labor Law,
President of TEP International.

More About Harris Jacobs and Katherine Stock:
Marriage: December 27, Rome, Georgia

Children of Harris Jacobs and Katherine Stock are:

1. Faye Ellen Jacobs, born September 30, 1956 in Atlanta, Georgia; married (1) Sammy Twisdale; married (2) Ken Taylor in Atlanta; married (3) John Kent in Atlanta.

3 ii. Marsha Ruth Jacobs, born October 29, 1958 in Atlanta, Georgia; married Larry Walter Freudenberg September 06, 1981 in Atlanta, Georgia.

iii. Charles Brian Jacobs, born November 16, 1962 in Atlanta, Georgia; married Delia Harris October 22, 1994 in Atlanta, Georgia; born February 06, 1959 in Jacksonville, Florida.

Generation No. 4

8. Walter Freudenberg born March 23, 1890 in Essen, Germany; died December 31, 1952 in KKBE Huguenin Avenue. He was the son of **16. Heynemann Freudenberg** and **17. Bertha Buschoff.** He married **9. Margot Strauss** June 12, 1928 in Essen, Germany.

9. Margot Strauss born August 08, 1907 in Hanover, Germany. She was the daughter of **18. Dr. Henry Strauss** and **19. Ella Ganz**.

More About Walter Freudenberg:
Burial: Charleston, South Carolina KKBE Huguenin Avenue Cemetery
Emigration: June 23, 1939, Emigrated to United Kingdom

Notes for Margot Strauss:

Tuesday, December 29, 1998 ***Charleston Post & Courier*** *Article by Elsa McDowell*

LOCAL "TREASURE" IS NOW TRULY TIME-HONORED

"If you were distracted by holiday haste, you might have missed Time magazine's recent tribute to Margot Strauss Freudenberg. But if you have been in the Lowcountry long enough to know a cancer patient or to attend a symphony concert or to encounter an international visitor in distress, you likely can guess what it says. It says Margot Freudenberg is a Charleston treasure. It says she is no less a legend than Rainbow Row or Fort Sumter. (All right. It says "Fort Sumter," but we'll forgive the editor in light of what else the article says.) It says that Margot Freudenberg is "a real star" in the area of   second careers. You probably knew that. But it is awfully nice for 750,000 households to know it, even folks in Wyoming know now is that more than 40 years ago, Mrs. Freudenberg started a Foreign Language Interpreters' List to provide free emergency translation services to hospitals, police and   schools. In Alabama, they know that, at 91, she continues to provide the service whereby 200 translators offer assistance in 53 foreign

languages. From 1957 ... Rhode Islanders know the story of how it started: A doctor couldn't communicate with his critically ill patient, a Dutch sailor. He enlisted help from Mrs. Freudenberg, a physical therapist and a German immigrant. But the sailor couldn't understand her German any better than the doctor's English. Freudenberg made a public appeal for someone to help and a Dutchman working in town responded. The patient's illness was diagnosed as multiple sclerosis and he was flown home to Holland. The idea that foreigners could die in local hospitals because of language barriers haunted her. So, within a few months, she had put together a list of interpreters. In New Mexico, Time readers know about her success. Thousands of people have been helped by Mrs. Freudenberg's work - Cuban boat people stranded in port; Mexican migrant workers who couldn't communicate with hospital staff about their illnesses; Vietnamese school children who couldn't understand instructions; and a Norwegian sailor who ran away from a hospital because he was afraid his ship would leave without him. ... until today. And in Germany, the country Mrs. Freudenberg fled during World War II with her Jewish parents, husband and son, Henry, Time has put it on record that she is happy to help people in distress as a way of repaying her debt to the United States. What those readers will not know is that her adopted home many years ago moved from the creditors' column to the debtors' column in its relationship with Margot Freudenberg. The Medical University of South Carolina tried to even the score by giving her a Doctor of Humane Letters degree in 1990. The Trident Community Foundation did its part by awarding her its Malcolm D. Haven award for "unselfish contributions and accomplishments."The National Council of Jewish Women in 1992 gave her the Hannah G. Solomon Award for her valor, faith and humanity. And the Daughters of the American Revolution made her the first naturalized American citizen to receive its Americanism Medal. But by my computations, we *still are in arrears to Mrs. Freudenberg. It is not, after all, just life-saving interpreters that she has provided. Beyond words... It is support for the American Cancer Society. She helped establish a cancer clinic for women here in the mid-1950s and a new facility where patients from out of town can stay for $5 a night. She helped found the Hope School in 1959 for the benefit of mentally handicapped. She was a record-setting fund-raiser for the Heart Fund. She volunteered with the Chamber of Commerce. She has given her energy for the Charleston Symphony Orchestra for more than 50 years. And I can attest personally that she has provided inspiration for and given encouragement to scores of individuals. So, thank you, Time, for honoring Margot Freudenberg. And, Mrs. Freudenberg? Danke. Merci. Grazie. Dekuji vam. Gracias. Asante sana. Todah rabah."*

More About Walter Freudenberg and Margot Strauss:
Marriage: June 12, 1928, Essen, Germany

Child of Walter Freudenberg and Margot Strauss is:

4   i.   Henry Heineman Freudenberg, born April 02, 1929 in Essen, Germany; married Maxine Anne Triest January 07, 1951 in Charleston, South Carolina.

10.   Maier Triest He was the son of **20. Montague Triest** and **21. Adelaide Israel**. He married **11. Miriam Hendricks Neuberger** May 03, 1925 in Augusta, Georgia.
11.   Miriam Hendricks Neuberger, born July 26, 1905 in Augusta, GA; died June 18, 2001 in Charleston , SC, She was the daughter of **22. Max H. Neuberger** and **23. Rosina Levy.**

29

Notes for Maier Triest:
By Larry Freudenberg & Dale Rosengarten.
3/26/2001
Dale Rosengarten, PhD
Curator, Jewish Heritage Collection
Robert Scott Small Library
College of Charleston

A fourth-generation Charlestonian and consummate southerner, Maier Triest's one regret was that his mother traveled to see family in New York late in her pregnancy and he was born in the North instead of at home. He grew up in a large house in the heart of Charleston, near the old mill pond now known as Colonial Lake. With his two younger sisters and friends, Maier would paddle the pond in small wooden boats. Charlestonians who could afford it spent summers at the beach for relief from the heat and humidity. The Triests would escape to Sullivan's Island, across the Cooper River from the city. A graduate of The High School of Charleston, Maier attended his father's Alma mater, Columbia University, in New York City, close to relatives on both sides of the family. He transferred and graduated from the College of Charleston. Upon graduation he went to work with his father and uncle in their family insurance, real estate, and auction business, Triest & Israel, on Broad Street in Charleston. Maier was twenty-six and had just married Miriam Neuberger of Augusta when his father died suddenly of a heart attack, thrusting upon him responsibility for managing the family's business and personal affairs.

Maier's great-grandparents, Joseph and Caroline

Triest, had emigrated from the Kingdom of Bavaria with their son, the first Maier, around 1850. This Maier was thirty years old and a captain in the militia (Triest's Company, Beat 2) when the Civil War began.

In January 1862 he enlisted in the 24th South Carolina volunteers, and a year later was promoted from Sergeant Major to Regimental Quartermaster Sergeant. His job was to supply the regiment with shoes, clothing, blankets, cooking utensils, etc. In 1869 he married German-born Hannah Reichman in Cincinnati and in 1871 both he and his father Joseph became American citizens in the South Carolina District Court. Triest's service to the Confederacy was typical of German immigrants of the period, as was his family's allegiance to Reform Judaism and Beth Elohim. The second Maier Triest served as president of the congregation and president of Charleston's B'nai B'rith. He was a founder of B'nai B'rith's first youth chapter for boys (AZA) in Charleston, southeastern district secretary for B'nai B'rith, president of the Hebrew Orphan Society and president of the Hebrew Benevolent Societies. In addition Maier was active in civic affairs. He chaired the Charleston County School Board, belonged to the Elks Club and the Hibernian Society, served on the board of South Carolina Electric and Gas, and was a founder and board member of Home Federal Savings & Loan. Later in life, Maier was a guest writer for the Charleston News & Courier, reporting on his travels to Canada and Europe. Maier had one child, Maxine Anne Triest, and three grandchildren. Maxine's husband, Henry H. Freudenberg, was a Holocaust survivor who met Maxine when they were just eleven years old, at a dinner party at the Triest home. Maier

Triest died of cancer at the age of sixty-seven and was buried in the Coming Street cemetery.

More About Maier Triest:
Awards: 1967, Commended by the SC General Assembly for service to the county and state.
Cause of Death: Cancer. Started in pancreas
Cemetery: April 25, 1969, Coming Street Cemetery
Medical Information: Diabetic. Type II
Stone: April 25, 1969, *I Shall Pass Through This World but Once. If, therefore, there be any kindness I can show or any good thing I can do, Let me do it now. For I shall not pass this way again.*
Synagogue: Kahal Kadosh Beth Elohim, Charleston
Undergraduate: 1921, Attended Columbia University and then the College of Charleston.

Notes for Miriam Hendricks Neuberger:
We called our grandmother, "Momoo". This was a name given to her by my oldest sister, Lynn. Miriam loved to travel. With my grandfather, Maier they traveled to many countries. On her travels she collected dolls and in Mexico collected statues of wood by a Mexican artist, Penal. After Maier died in 1969, Miriam continued to travel including a trip to Africa and a trip every December to Mexico. She was devoted to her half brother, Simon Sorentrue.

About Miriam Hendricks Neuberger:
Cemetery: June 20, 2001, Coming Street Cemetery
Medical Information: Alzheimer's disease at age 84 (1989).
Undergraduate: University of Georgia, Athens, Georgia

32

More About Maier Triest and Miriam Neuberger:
Marriage: May 03, 1925, Augusta, Georgia

Child of Maier Triest and Miriam Neuberger is:
    5 i. Maxine Anne Triest, born September 14, 1930 in Charleston, South Carolina; married Henry Heineman Freudenberg January 07, 1951 in Charleston, South Carolina.

    12. **Joseph Jacobs,** born July 15, 1908 in Birmingham, Alabama; died June 29, 1998 in Atlanta, Georgia. He married **13. Esther Rosenwald** 1928 in West Palm Beach, Florida.
    13. **Esther Rosenwald,** born September 1900 in Springfield, MA; died 1985 in Atlanta, Georgia. She was the daughter of **26. Harris G. Rosenwald** and **27. Julia Cassell.**

More About Joseph Jacobs: (by Julian Jacobs)
Senior Labor Law Attorney in the Southeast
Graduate: Atlanta School of Law
Involved in historic textile strikes in the South during the tumultuous thirties.
Expelled the KKK from the historic Wigwam building in Atlanta during the 1940's.
Rented at the Wigwam building to the first racially integrated Veterans group after WWII (American Veterans Committee).
Leader in the Democratic Party in Georgia.
Delegate to Presidential Conventions.
Lover of the Yiddish Language.

More about Esther Rosenwald: (by Julian Jacobs)
Supported Joseph Jacobs in Law School

Plagued by Psychiatric illness but successfully raised three sons

Children of Joseph Jacobs and Esther Rosenwald are:

    6 i. Harris Jacobs, born May 21, 1930 in Atlanta, Georgia; died December 22, 1993 in Atlanta, Georgia; married Katherine Rae Stock December 27 in Rome, Georgia.

        ii. Julian Jacobs, born November 05, 1932 in Atlanta, Georgia; married (1) Norma Claire Glazer March 18, 1956 in Atlanta, Georgia at Mayfair Club; born July 20, 1935 in Atlanta, Georgia; died October 28, 1992 in Atlanta, Georgia; married (2) Eleanor Pollock January 19, 1997 in Or VeShalom Synagogue, Atlanta, GA; born December 02, 1934 in Williamsport, Pa.

More About Julian Jacobs: (by Julian Jacobs)
Medical Information: Heart condition. Bypass surgery. Type II diabetic.
Graduate Cornell Medical School
AB Cornell University
MD Emory University School of Medicine
Professor of Medicine Emeritus Emory University School of Medicine
Chief Hematology /Medical Oncology VA Medical Center Atlanta, Three decades
Lover of Hebrew Language

More About Norma Claire Glazer: (by Julian Jacobs)
Cause of Death: leukemia
Summa Cum Laude graduate of Boston University School of Fine Arts (Piano and Music Education)
Piano Student of Ernst Bacon at BU

Lover of the Jewish People and the State of Israel
Taught Piano, Jewish and General Music, Hebrew for
over three decades in Atlanta
First Music Teacher in Pioneer town of Arad, Israel

More About Julian Jacobs and Norma Glazer:
Marriage: March 18, 1956, Atlanta, Georgia at Mayfair
Club

More about Eleanor Pollock: (by Julian Jacobs)
First cousin of Norma Glazer (were more like sisters
according to Julian Jacobs)
Graduate Syracuse University
Teacher and Travel Agent

iii. Leonard Jacobs, born November 03, 1935
in Atlanta, Georgia; died June 30, 1965 in Atlanta,
Georgia; married Gloria Merie Buchsbaum April 20,
1958 in Savannah, GA. Reception at the Desoto
Hotel; born March 18, 1939 in Savannah, GA at
Telfair Hospital/Savannah, Chatham Co., GA.

Notes for Leonard Jacobs:
Beloved by his friends and family
Graduate University of Georgia
Lover of Athletics
A Free spirit
Youngest brother of Harris & Julian Jacobs, Lenny
married Gloria Buschbaum of Savannah and had two
daughters. Lenny died of a massive heart attack when
his kids were only 5 and 3 years old. Outgoing and
athletic. He sold life insurance and as loved by his
family.

14. Casper Isadore Stock (Source: Larry W.

Freudenberg, Rodeph Sholom cemetery Rome, GA.),
born January 02, 1897 in Mt. Vernon, New
York/Mount Vernon, Erie Co., NY; died September
28, 1982 in Rome, Georgia. He was the son of **28.
Charles Stock** and **29. Anna Taschman**. He
married **15. Sarah Francis Esserman** 1922.

    15. Sarah Francis Esserman (Source: Larry W.
Freudenberg, Rodeph Sholom Cemetery Rome, GA.),
born July 15, 1900 in Rome, Georgia; died May 08,
1988 in Rome, Georgia. She was the daughter of **30.
Joseph Esserman** and **31. Fannie Mendelson**.

Notes for Casper Isadore Stock:
Yahrzeit Plaque at Rodeph Sholom Temple in Rome,
GA.
Hebrew name on plaque. Casper ben Tishreles.
Hebrew name: Katriel Yitzchak ben Tishreles.

More About Casper Isadore Stock:
Cemetery: Rodeph Sholom Cemetery
Stone: *My Beloved Husband and Our Dear Father*

Notes for Sarah Francis Esserman:
Yahrzeit plaque at Rodeph Sholom in Rome, GA.
Sarah bat Yoseph.

More About Sarah Francis Esserman:
Cemetery: Rodeph Sholom cemetery
Stone: *A Beloved Wife and Our Dear Mother*

Children of Casper Stock and Sarah Esserman are:
       i.   Louise Shirley Stock, born November 11,
1923 in Rome, Georgia; married Murray Stein
September 05, 1948 in Rome, Georgia; born June 02,
1924 in Savannah, GA.

ii. Joseph David Stock (Source: Larry W. Freudenberg, Rodeph Sholom Cemetery Rome, GA.), born December 07, 1927 in Rome, Georgia; died November 22, 1991 in Rome, Georgia; married Dorothy Rose Simmons in Atlanta, Georgia; born February 03, 1932 in Macon, Georgia/Macon Co., GA.

Notes for Joseph David Stock:
Yahrzeit Plaque at Rodeph Sholom Temple in Rome, GA.
Yoseph David ben Katriel Yitzchak.

More About Joseph David Stock:
Cemetery: Rodeph Sholom cemetery
Stone: *His Legacy. Kindness. Charity. Optimism.*

7   iii. Katherine Rae Stock, born June 21, 1931 in Rome, Georgia; married Harris Jacobs December 27 in Rome, Georgia.

Generation No. 5

16.   Heynemann Freudenberg (Source: *Mourning Book of Heynemann Freudenberg*, (Includes newspaper articles, obituaries, condolence letters).), born July 06, 1853 in Lippstadt, Essen, Germany/Essen, Germany; died May 12, 1928 in Essen, Germany. He was the son of **32. Abraham Freudenberg**. He married **17. Bertha Buschoff** in Hanover, Germany.
17.   Bertha Buschoff, born December 15, 1857 in Xantan on the Rhine, Germany; died May 15, 1939

37

in Essen, Germany. She was the daughter of **34. Simon Buschoff** and **35. Helene Fischbein**.

More About Heynemann Freudenberg:
Died of pneumonia
Stone: May 12, 1928, Grave Stone. *ER HT DA BEST. FUR DIE SEINEN UND STIFTETE FRIEDEN FUR SEIN*

More About Bertha Buschoff:

Burial: May 15, 1939, Essen, Germany

More About Heynemann Freudenberg and Bertha Buschoff:

Marriage: Hanover, Germany

Children of Heynemann Freudenberg and Bertha Buschoff are:
      i. Arthur Freudenberg, born September 27, 1880 in Essen, Germany; died 1945 in London, England; married Anne Virneau; born June 12, 1888 in Essen, Germany.

More About Arthur Freudenberg:
Lived in England. Had a son from non Jewish spouse, Anna Virnace

      ii. Hedwig Freudenberg, born December 12, 1882 in Essen, Germany; died 1953 in Basel, Switzerland; married Leo Lehmann; born January 12, 1871 in Pasewalk, Germany.

More About Hedwig Freudenberg:
1953, Died in Basel, Switzerland

8   iii. Walter Freudenberg, born March 23, 1890 in Essen, Germany; died December 31, 1952 in KKBE Huguenin Avenue; married Margot Strauss June 12, 1928 in Essen, Germany.

18.   Dr. Henry Strauss (Source: KKBE Huguenin Avenue cemetery.), born May 30, 1873 in Markbrait, Bravaria, Germany; died August 24, 1947 in Charleston, South Carolina. He was the son of **36. Jacob Strauss** and **37. Getti Spatz**. He married **19. Ella Ganz** October 29, 1902 in Hanover.
    19.   Ella Ganz (Source: KKBE Huguenin Avenue cemetery.), born December 04, 1881 in Bunde, Westphalia, Germany; died April 04, 1962 in Charleston, South Carolina. She was the daughter of **38. Alex Ganz** and **39. Berta Stern**.

Notes for Dr. Henry Strauss:
Left Germany in 1937 with his wife, Ella. Settled in England with Henry's brothers, Justin and Sigfried. Left England in October of 1940 for Greenville, SC to live with his daughter, Hilda. When Hilda was ill with brain tumors, Henry & Ella left Greenville to live with daughter, Margot in Charleston, SC.

Children of Henry Strauss and Ella Ganz are:
    i.   Hilda Strauss, born December 05, 1903 in Hanover, Germany; died November 27, 1945 in Greenville, South Carolina (USA); married Ludwig Rothschild.
    9   ii. Margot Strauss, born August 08, 1907 in Hanover, Germany; married Walter Freudenberg June

12, 1928 in Essen, Germany.

20. Montague Triest (Source: (1) Coming Street Cemetery., (2) Larry W. Freudenberg, Interview with Caroline Louise Triest, 1990's in Charleston.), born September 02, 1871 in Charleston, South Carolina; died August 22, 1927 in Charleston , SC (Source: Barnett Elzas, *The Old Jewish Cemeteries at Charleston, SC,* (The Daggett Printing Company 1903).). He was the son of **40. Maier Triest** and **41. Hannah Reichman**. He married **21. Adelaide Israel** November 08, 1898 in Charleston, SC Married at home. by revised. B.A. Elzas. The News & Courier, 11/15/98.

21. Adelaide Israel (Source: (1) Coming Street Cemetery., (2) Larry W. Freudenberg, Interview with Adelaide Jacobs née Triest, 1990's in Charleston.), born November 04, 1876 in Charleston, South Carolina; died October 05, 1960 in Charleston , SC (Source: Barnett Elzas, *The Old Jewish Cemeteries at Charleston, SC,* (The Daggett Printing Company 1903).). She was the daughter of **42. Morris Israel** and **43. Rebecca Elias**.

Notes for Montague Triest:
Montague Triest started our family's business in 1903 as Triest & Israel. The business started as an insurance agency with his brother in law, Melvin Israel. Melvin left the business in the 1920's and later committed suicide in 1931 in New York.

Montague was a respected business person in Charleston. He was considered a "gentlemen". A copy of his obituary is in the family archives and will be a part of his scrapbook. His three children are Maier, Adelaide and Caroline. Maier joined his family in the family business after graduating from Columbia College. Adelaide married Samuel H. Jacobs and Caroline never married.

Montague was called "Mr. Mont". He was very active in Charleston civic organizations including the Elks. Montague died at the age of 55 of an apparent heart attack. At the time Caroline was finishing library science school at Emory University in Atlanta, Adelaide was married and Maier was working at the business.

More About Montague Triest:
Cause of Death: heart attack or stroke. Sudden death.
Cemetery: August 22, 1927, Coming Street
Stone: August 22, 1927, *A Prince and a great man hath fallen this day in Israel*

More About Adelaide Israel:
Cemetery: October 04, 1960, Coming Street
Stone: October 05, 1960, *She live on in the acts of kindness she performed and in the hearts of those who cherish her memories*

More About Montague Triest and Adelaide Israel:
Marriage: November 08, 1898, Charleston, SC Married at home. by revised. B.A. Elzas (Rabbi of Kahal Kadosh Beth Elohim).
Marriage date: Married at Adelaide's parent's home at 54 Wentworth Street, Charleston, SC.

Children of Montague Triest and Adelaide Israel are:
    10 i.   Maier Triest, born July 26, 1901 in New

York City, New York; died April 25, 1969 in Charleston , SC; married Miriam Hendricks Neuberger May 03, 1925 in Augusta, Georgia.

ii. Adelaide Rebecca Triest (Source: Coming Street Cemetery.), born July 29, 1905 in Charleston, South Carolina; died August 14, 1998 in Charleston , SC (Source: Barnett Elzas, *The Old Jewish Cemeteries at Charleston, SC*, (The Daggett Printing Company 1903).); married Samuel Hyams Jacobs June 21, 1927 in Charleston, South Carolina; born July 02, 1905 in 510 King Street, Charleston, SC; died September 04, 1989 in Charleston , SC (Source: Barnett Elzas, *The Old Jewish Cemeteries at Charleston, SC*, (The Daggett Printing Company 1903).).

Notes for Adelaide Rebecca Triest:
Born at 1 o'clock Saturday. Private book of her mother. Aunt Adelaide was visiting Maxine's home for lunch on August 14, 1998 and collapsed soon after arriving. Larry, Maxine and Henry were with her when she died. Adelaide lived a life of peace and happiness with many wonderful years with her beloved husband, Sammy, she died without any pain. Her sister, Caroline L. Triest said on the night of her death that she was grateful that Adelaide died peacefully and did not suffer.

More About Adelaide Rebecca Triest:
Cause of Death: old age
Cemetery: Coming Street Cemetery
Medical Information: diabetic. Type II. heart disease in her 80's. pacemaker.
Place of Death: August 14, 1998, Adelaide died of old age at 93 at the home of Maxine Triest Freudenberg
Stone: A Caring Lady

Undergraduate: 1927, Graduate. College of Charleston. Major in Chemistry.

More About Samuel Hyams Jacobs:
Birth Certificate: March 07, 1957, Certificate of Birth. County of Charleston. 67/533
Cemetery: Coming Street Cemetery
Stone: A Gentle Man

More About Samuel Jacobs and Adelaide Triest:
Marriage: June 21, 1927, Charleston, South Carolina
Marriage date: Married at the Francis Marion Hotel in Charleston

iii. Caroline Louise Triest (Source: Coming Street Cemetery.), born June 23, 1907 in Charleston, South Carolina; died July 18, 2002 in Charleston , SC (Source: Barnett Elzas, *The Old Jewish Cemeteries at Charleston, SC,* (The Daggett Printing Company 1903).).

More About Caroline Louise Triest:
Cemetery: Coming Street Cemetery
Graduate Degree: 1931, Graduate Bachelors of Arts in Library Science. Emory
Undergraduate: 1928, Graduate College of Charleston

22.   Max H. Neuberger (Source: Magnolia Cemetery. Tombstone)**,** born May 27, 1878 in Savannah, Georgia; died July 20, 1906 in Tybee Beach, Savannah, Georgia (Source: Magnolia Cemetery.). He was the son of **44. Herman Neuberger** and **45. Miriam.** He married **23. Rosina Levy** October 30, 1904 in Augusta, Georgia.

23. Rosina Levy (Source: (1) Malcolm H. Stern, *First American Jewish Families - 600 Genealogies - 1654 - 1988*, (Ottenheimer Publishers; 3rd Ed. updated and revised edition (1988)), 167., (2) KKBE Huguenin Avenue Cemetery., (3) Malcolm H. Stern, *Americans of Jewish Descent: A Compendium of Genealogy* , (Hebrew Union College Press, Cincinnati; 1st edition (1960)), 116.), born September 05, 1884 in Blackville, South Carolina; died August 12, 1972 in Charleston , SC (Source: KKBE Huguenin Avenue Cemetery.). She was the daughter of **46. Jacob H. Levy** and **47. Annie Brown**.

More About Max H. Neuberger:
Cemetery: July 21, 1906, Augusta, GA, Magnolia Cemetery, Walton Way Temple, Children of Israel
Stone: July 20, 1906, Drowned in surf at Tybee Beach, SC

More About Rosina Levy:
Cemetery: August 14, 1972, KKBE Huguenin Avenue

More About Max Neuberger and Rosina Levy:
Marriage: October 30, 1904, Augusta, Georgia

Child of Max Neuberger and Rosina Levy is:
11 i. Miriam Hendricks Neuberger, born July 26, 1905 in Augusta, GA; died June 18, 2001 in Charleston , SC; married Maier Triest May 03, 1925 in Augusta, Georgia.

25. Sarah Jacobs

Children of Sarah Jacobs are:

12 i. Joseph Jacobs, born July 15, 1908 in Birmingham, AL; died June 29, 1998 in Atlanta, Georgia at Workman's Circle Section; married (1) Temaley Yett in Atlanta, Georgia; married (2) Mary Andrews; married (3) Esther Rosenwald 1928 in West Palm Beach, Florida.

ii. Alex Jacobs, died May 01, 1998; married Dora Shymlock.

iii. Henrietta Jacobs, married Boris Bell.

iv. Ann Jacobs, married Al Wacksman.

26. Harris G. Rosenwald, born in Poland Russia/Poland. He married **27. Julia Cassell.**

27. Julia Cassell, born in Nurenburg, Germany.

Notes for Harris G. Rosenwald:
Original United States Citizenship paper. December 20, 1890 by the Circuit Court of Mass. District. SS. "Harris G. Rosenwald of South Boston in said District , Merchant born at Poland Russia having produced the evidence and taken oath required by law, was admitted to become a citizen of the said United States according to the Acts of Congress in such case made and provided."

Original in possession of Kitty Jacobs at 1563 Beachcliff Drive, Atlanta, GA.

More About Harris G. Rosenwald:
December 20, 1890, Citizenship awarded by Circuit Court of United States, Mass. District. SS

Children of Harris Rosenwald and Julia Cassell are:

13 i. Esther Rosenwald, born September 1900 in Springfield, MA; died 1985 in Atlanta, Georgia at Workman's Circle Section; married Joseph Jacobs 1928 in West Palm Beach, Florida.

ii. Blanche Rosenwald

iii. Fannie Rosenwald, married Ben Ryder.

iv. Pearl Rosenwald, married Justin Held; died in Atlanta, Georgia.

v. Ettabinah Rosenwald

vi. Muriel Rosenwald, died in MA; married Myron Sandler.

vii. Lillie Rosenwald

viii. Eddie Rosenwald

ix. Maurice Rosenwald

28.   Charles Stock (Source: Larry W. Freudenberg, Rodeph Sholom Cemetery Rome, GA.), born January 01, 1870 in Plotz, Poland; died November 09, 1948 in Rome, Georgia. He married **29. Anna Taschman**.

29.   Anna Taschman, born in Plotz, Poland; died in Rome, Georgia.

More About Charles Stock:
Cemetery: Rodeph Sholom Cemetery

Children of Charles Stock and Anna Taschman are:

i. Fannie Stock

ii. Eva Stock (Source: Larry W. Freudenberg, Rodeph Sholom Cemetery Rome, GA.), born March 15, 1889 in New York City, New York; died October 27, 1970 in Savannah, GA; married a man named Kantziper (first name unknown).

More About Eva Stock:
Cemetery: Rodeph Sholom Cemetery
Stone: Her Love for Her Children Was Always in Her Thoughts. Beloved By All Who Knew Her. May Our Merciful God Give Her Shalom

    14 iii.   Casper Isadore Stock, born January 02, 1897 in Mt. Vernon, New York/Mount Vernon, Erie Co., NY; died September 28, 1982 in Rome, Georgia; married Sarah Francis Esserman 1922.
    iv.   Sarah Ruth Stock (Source: Larry W. Freudenberg, Rodeph Sholom Cemetery Rome, GA.), born September 05, 1899; died October 01, 1955 in Rome, Georgia; married Weinberg.

More About Sarah Ruth Stock:
Cemetery: Rodeph Sholom Cemetery

    v.   Samuel Moses Stock (Source: Larry W. Freudenberg, Rodeph Sholom Cemetery Rome, GA.), born January 03, 1902; died December 06, 1946 in Rome, Georgia.

More About Samuel Moses Stock:
Cemetery: Rodeph Sholom Cemetery

    30.   Joseph Esserman (Source: Larry W. Freudenberg, Rodeph Sholom Cemetery Rome, GA.), born 1872; died May 27, 1927 in Rome, Georgia. He was the son of **60. David Esserman**. He married **31. Fannie Mendelson**.
    31.   Fannie Mendelson, born 1872; died February 26, 1941 in Rome, Georgia.

More About Joseph Esserman:
Cemetery: May 27, 1927, Rodeph Sholom Cemetery

Children of Joseph Esserman and Fannie Mendelson are:

      i.   Hattie Esserman (Source: Larry W. Freudenberg, Rodeph Sholom Cemetery Rome, GA.), born November 22, 1898; died 1997 in Rome, Georgia; married David Morris Rives; died in Rome, Georgia.

    15 ii. Sarah Francis Esserman, born July 15, 1900 in Rome, Georgia; died May 08, 1988 in Rome, Georgia; married Casper Isadore Stock 1922.

      iii. Ida Esserman (Source: Larry W. Freudenberg, Rodeph Sholom Cemetery Rome, GA.), born November 22, 1904; died January 12, 1990 in Rome, Georgia; married Reiner.

Notes for Ida Esserman:
Yahrzeit plaque at Rodeph Sholom Temple in Rome, GA, Ida bat Yoseph

More About Ida Esserman:
Cemetery: January 12, 1990, Rodeph Sholom Cemetery
Stone: Beloved Daughter

Generation No. 6

32.   Abraham Freudenberg, born 1818 in Germany, Boedefeld; died November 14, 1863. He was the son of **64. Heineman Freudenberg**.

Children of Abraham Freudenberg are:

16 i. Heynemann Freudenberg, born July 06, 1853 in Lippstadt, Essen, Germany/Essen, Germany; died May 12, 1928 in Essen, Germany; married Bertha Buschoff in Hanover, Germany.

  ii. Louis Freudenberg, born May 09, 1855 in Lippstadt, Essen, Germany/Essen, Germany; died 1943 in Teresin (Theresienstadt) Concentration Camp; married Ernestine Lieberg; born September 03, 1871 in Kassel; died August 1936 in Essen, Germany.

More About Ernestine Lieberg:
Freeman: Her daughter Gertrud died of pemphigus a year later.
Died of a rare virus: Pemphigus

34. Simon Buschoff, born 1809 in Essen, Germany; died 1864 in Xanten, Germany. He married **35. Helene Fischbein.**

35. Helene Fischbein, born November 29, 1820 in Essen, Germany; died June 10, 1900. She was the daughter of **70. Leser Fischbein** and **71. Sophie Vogelsang**.

Children of Simon Buschoff and Helene Fischbein are:

  i. Karl Buschoff, born in Xanten, Germany; died in Essen, Germany.

  ii. Sigmund Buschoff, born February 24, 1851; died July 20, 1922 in Bochum, Germany; married Nettchen; born July 24, 1847 in Bochum, Germany; died July 05, 1915 in Bochum, Germany.

  iii. Julius Buschoff, born May 21, 1855 in Xanten, Germany; died November 18, 1928 in

Worms, Germany.

17 iv. Bertha Buschoff, born December 15, 1857 in Xantan on the Rhine, Germany; died May 15, 1939 in Essen, Germany; married Heynemann Freudenberg in Hanover, Germany.

v. Nettchen Buschoff, born December 22, 1861 in Xanten, Germany; died January 01, 1920 in Essen, Germany; married Bernard Schuster; born October 07, 1853 in Lugde, Germany; died July 30, 1899 in Philadelphia, PA.

36. Jacob Strauss, born November 19, 1846 in Geroldshausen, Germany; died November 17, 1913 in Frankfurt, Germany. He married **37. Getti Spatz.**

37. Getti Spatz, born May 30, 1850 in Bishberg near Bamberg, Germany; died March 21, 1920.

Children of Jacob Strauss and Getti Spatz are:

i. Justin Strauss, died 1940 in London, England; married Millia Kuhn; born in Landau, Germany.

ii. Leo Strauss, died in Capetown, South Africa.

iii. Sigfried Strauss, born 1871; married Paula Bloch; born in Marktbreit, Germany.

18 iv. Dr. Henry Strauss, born May 30, 1873 in Markbrait, Bravaria, Germany; died August 24, 1947 in Charleston, South Carolina; married Ella Ganz October 29, 1902 in Hanover.

v. Hugo Strauss, born 1875 in Marktbreit, Germany; died 1931 in Frankfurt; married Ricka Frankenfelder; born 1885 in Heidingsfeld, Southern Germany; died 1965 in Tel Aviv, Israel.

38. Alex Ganz, born 1848 in Bunde, Westphalia, Germany; died 1921 in Hanover, Germany. He was the son of **76. Leser Ganz** and **77. Eva Levisohn.** He married **39. Berta Stern.**

39. Berta Stern, born 1860 in Geseke, Germany; died 1934 in Hanover, Germany. She was the daughter of **78. Aaron Stern** and **79. Emile Loewenbach.**

Children of Alex Ganz and Berta Stern are:

19 i. Ella Ganz, born December 04, 1881 in Bunde, Westphalia, Germany; died April 04, 1962 in Charleston, South Carolina; married Dr. Henry Strauss October 29, 1902 in Hanover.

ii. Otto Ganz, died in Victim of Holocaust; married Gerta September 12, 1907 in Germany, Aachen.

iii. Paul Ganz, married Grete Stern January 18, 1920 in Aachen, Germany.

More About Paul Ganz and Grete Stern:
Marriage: January 18, 1920, Aachen, Germany

40. Maier Triest (Source: (1) Coming Street Cemetery., (2) Robert N. Rosen, **The Jewish Confederates,** (University of SC Press 2000)., (3) Thomas J. Tobias, *Tombstones That Tell Stories,* (Revised by Solomon Breibart 2000)., (4) Confederate Veteren., (5) Eugene W. Jones Jr., **Enlisted for the War - The Struggles of the Gallant 24th Regiment, SC Volunteers, Infantry 1861-1865,** (Longstreet House 1997).**),** born August 09, 1831 in

Germany, Kingdom of Bavaria; died August 18, 1894 in Charleston , SC (Source: Barnett Elzas, **The Old Jewish Cemeteries at Charleston, SC**, (The Daggett Printing Company 1903).). He was the son of **80. Joseph Triest** and **81. Caroline Hollander**. He married **41. Hannah Reichman** February 10, 1869 in Ohio, Cincinnati.

    41.   **Hannah Reichman,** born 1849 in Bookenheim, Germany; died September 02, 1929 in New York City, New York. She was the daughter of **82. Raphael Reichman** and **83. Frances**.

Notes for Maier Triest:

Maier Triest, whose family had come from Bavaria in the early part of the 19th century, was born in 1831. He was thirty years old when the war (Civil War) started and served as Captain of Triest's Col. (Beat 2), 16th SC Militia from November 9 to December 20, 1861. As most young, able-bodied Charlestonians served in a militia unit prior to the war, Triest undoubtedly served in one such organization as this company bears his name, and he served as Captain. In January, 1862, Triest and hundreds of other South Carolinians enlisted in the 24th SC Volunteers, a regiment raised by Colonel Clement H. Steven, who had formerly commanded Triest's militia regiment and may have known Triest prior to that time. The 24th was originally organized by Stevens and Lt Colonel Ellison Capers for twelve months of Confederate service. Six companies were raised for one year when state policy changed in March, 1862, to require service for the duration of the war. All the men agreed to so serve. (Rivers Account of the Raising of Troops in South Carolina for State and Confederate Service 1861 - 1865, Columbia, SC, The

Bryan Publishing Company, 1899, pages. 29-30,)

Colonel Stevens chose Triest to be Sergeant-Major of the 24th SC, whereupon Triest re-enlisted at that rank on January 20, 1862 (C.S.R.). In January, 1863, he was promoted to Regimental Quartermaster Sergeant, a position he held throughout the war. Rabbi Elzas (who, of course, knew Triest and his family) wrote that Triest was "promoted twice to A.A.A. General [ASK Col. GABEL], once by General Stevens, who died before commission was returned, and again by General Capers just before the close of the war." (p. 235) [The compiled service records neither corroborate nor contradict this statement].

The 24th saw action throughout the war at Secessionville (SC), Jackson, Mississippi (Vicksburg campaign), Atlanta, Franklin, Nashville and the Carolinas. Triest was with the 24th in the weeks before the final assault on Vicksburg, when Grant attempted to get between Vicksburg, the Confederate stronghold on the Mississippi River, and the Confederate forces at Jackson, a city and rail hub --- miles to the east of Vicksburg. The South Carolinians were determined to prevent Jackson from falling to Grant's army. The 24th was engaged in fierce, hand-to-hand combat with the 10th Missouri. At Wright's Farm, a ball hit Colonel Ellison Caper's horse and a number of men of the 24th were killed. Capers wrote afterwards that Triest had given him "a most welcomed drink of whiskey." It was the only time Capers said he ever took a drink during the war. (Enlisted for the War, The Struggles of the Gallant 24th Regiment, South Carolina Volunteers, 1861 - 1865), Eugene W. Jones, Jr. , Longstreet House,

Hightown, NJ, 1997; on Triest, see pages. 15, 91, 214; Capers letter dated May 17, 1863, South Carolina Library, USC).

As Regimental Quartermaster Sergeant, it was Triest's job to see to it that the entire regiment was supplied. During the Jackson campaign, for example, he traveled to Canton and Meridian, Mississippi, to obtain shoes and clothing which had been left behind in storage at the beginning of the campaign. He traveled throughout July and August, 1863, retrieving and transporting boxes of clothing, cooking utensils and supplies. In early October, 1863, while at Chickamauga, Tenn., Triest was sent to Columbia and Charleston by General Braxton Bragg to act as agent for the collection of winter clothes, blankets and other supplies from the SC Relief Association. He returned on October 28 having used his own funds for "drayage" (movement by wagon) and cooperage (crating) at stops along the way. (The funds were refunded to him.)

He surrendered with the consolidated and redesignated 16th/24th SC Regiment with General Joseph E. Johnston's Army on April 26, 1865. He was paroled on May 1. According to Elzas, Triest was wounded at Atlanta (235).

Reprinted by permission from Robert Rosen. Compiled by Rosen for a presentation to the Sisterhood at Kahal Kadosh Beth Elohim, October. 25, 1997.

More About Maier Triest:
Cause of Death: Natural

Cemetery: August 18, 1894, Coming Street Cemetery
Employment: 1890, Dry and fancy good, carpets, upholstery, 259 King Street. "Cohen & Triest"
Military service: November 09, 1861, Civil War -Captain of Triest's Co., 16th SC Militia (Source: Robert N. Rosen, **The Jewish Confederates**, (University of SC Press 2000), 125,126.)
Stone: August 18, 1891, "A devoted husband, a loving father, a sincere friend. May his pure life and charitable deeds gain him eternal rest."

More About Hannah Reichman:
Burial: New York, New York

More About Maier Triest and Hannah Reichman:
Marriage: February 10, 1869, Ohio, Cincinnati

Children of Maier Triest and Hannah Reichman are:
　　　i. Fannie Triest (Source: Malcolm H. Stern, **First American Jewish Families - 600 Genealogies - 1654 - 1988**, (Ottenheimer Publishers; 3rd Ed. updated and revised edition (1988)).), born November 21, 1869; died June 03, 1930; married Isaac A. Goldsmith September 04, 1889; died May 22, 1909.

More About Isaac Goldsmith and Fannie Triest:
Marriage: September 04, 1889

　　20　ii. Montague Triest, born September 02, 1871 in Charleston, South Carolina; died August 22, 1927 in Charleston , SC; married Adelaide Israel November 08, 1898 in Charleston, SC Married at home. by revised. B.A. Elzas. *The News & Courier*, 11/15/98.
　　　　iii. Etta Triest, born August 28, 1873; died

February 07, 1956.

     iv. Miriam Triest, born August 19, 1876; died March 31, 1946; married Lemuel Victorius April 17, 1905.

     v. Caroline Triest, born October 22, 1878; died November 07, 1943.

     vi. Rosina Triest, born September 08, 1881; died April 02, 1885 in Charleston, South Carolina, Coming Street.

More About Rosina Triest:
Stone: April 02, 1885, "To live in hearts we leave behind is not to die" on her stone at Coming Street

     42. **Morris Israel** (Source: (1) James William Hagy, **This Happy Land - The Jews of Colonial and Antebellum Charleston**, (The University of Alabama Press 1993), 335., (2) Barnett Elzas, **The Jews of South Carolina, from the Earliest Times to the Present Day**, (Copyright 1905. First Edition), 169,269,265., (3) Coming Street Cemetery.), born February 14, 1835 in Posen, Kingdom of Prussia (Source: Larry W. Freudenberg, Interview with Caroline Louise Triest, 1990's in Charleston.); died October 20, 1911 in New York, New York (Source: Barnett Elzas, **The Old Jewish Cemeteries at Charleston, SC**, (The Daggett Printing Company 1903).). He married **43. Rebecca Elias** August 10, 1859 in Abbyville, SC.

     43. **Rebecca Elias** (Source: (1) James William Hagy, **This Happy Land - The Jews of Colonial and Antebellum Charleston**, (The University of Alabama Press 1993), 335., (2) Coming Street Cemetery.), born October 16, 1839 in St. Augustine,

Florida (Source: Larry W. Freudenberg, Interview with Adelaide Jacobs née Triest, 1990's in Charleston.); died December 05, 1896 in Charleston , SC (Source: Barnett Elzas, **The Old Jewish Cemeteries at Charleston, SC**, (The Daggett Printing Company 1903).). She was the daughter of **86. Levy Elias** and **87. Rosa Lilienthal**.

Notes for Morris Israel:
President of KKBE in 1886 when the big earthquake hit. Banker and retailer.
Lived at 54 Wentworth Street in Charleston. Picture of home in Freudenberg archives. Home was destroyed. Adelaide and Montague were married at this home.

More About Morris Israel:
Cause of Death: Heart attack
Cemetery: October 21, 1911, Coming Street Cemetery
Stone: "At Rest"

Notes for Rebecca Elias:
There is a painting of Rebecca Triest née Elias at Triest & Sholk Agency in Charleston. The matching picture of her husband, Morris Israel is with the family of Edgar Cohen in VA. Adelaide told me a story that after she acquired the painting and had it in her home, there was a threat of a fire. She took the painting off the wall and in her haste, she accidently put her finger through the painting. The hole was at the bust. Adelaide Triest Jacobs' aunt, Carrie (Caroline) Israel Cohen would come to visit and Adelaide would hide the hole by putting her hand/arm over the area! Later the painting was repaired. The size is about 36" wide by 40 " high.

57

The sterling silver lamp (converted electric) at Larry Freudenberg's house is Rebecca's and a slip rocker at Maxine T. Freudenberg's house..

More About Rebecca Elias:
Burial: Coming Street Cemetery
Residence: 1839, First recorded year in SC
Stone: December 05, 1896, "At Rest"

More About Morris Israel and Rebecca Elias:
Marriage: August 10, 1859, Abbyville, SC

Children of Morris Israel and Rebecca Elias are:
     i. Baby Israel (Source: Coming Street Cemetery.), born 1860.
     ii. Rosa Israel, born 1862; died 1863.
     iii. Samuel Israel, born 1863; married Mathilda D. Grausman; born in Raliegh, NC.
     iv. Isidore Israel, born 1864; died 1925.
     v. Lewis Israel (Source: Coming Street Cemetery.), born February 11, 1867; died June 22, 1903 in Charleston, South Carolina.

More About Lewis Israel:
Cemetery: Coming Street Cemetery

     vi. Arthur Israel, born 1868; died 1931; married Jeanette Brown.
     vii. Baby Israel (Source: Coming Street Cemetery.), born July 04, 1869 in Charleston, South Carolina; died July 08, 1869 in Charleston, South Carolina.

More About Baby Israel:

Cemetery: July 08, 1869, Coming Street Cemetery

viii. Melvin Mulvey Israel, born June 22, 1870; died May 27, 1931 in New York City, New York (Source: KKBE Huguenin Avenue Cemetery.); married (1) Corina Florence Moses; born November 03, 1871; died May 14, 1903 in Charleston , SC (Source: KKBE Huguenin Avenue Cemetery.); married (2) Ellen Rosenbaum August 10; died in Huguenin, Avenue Cemetery.

Notes for Melvin Mulvey Israel:
Wife finds M.M. Israel shot dead in Hotel Apartment.

Melvin M. Israel, 57 years old, a retired insurance executive, shot and killed himself yesterday afternoon in his room at the Hotel Lombardy, 111 East Fifty-sixth Street. When Mr. Israel's wife returned to the hotel at 4:30pm she found him dead, a revolver clutched in his right hand. Henry Weinberg, Assistant Medical Examiner pronounced the death a clear cut case of suicide.

Mrs. Israel could give no reason for her husband's act. She said he was neither ill nor in straitened financial circumstances. He was a jovial disposition, she said. They had lived at the hotel several years and had no children.

From the Private book of Addie Israel Triest. **New York Times** 5/27/31

More About Melvin Israel and Ellen Rosenbaum:
Marriage: August 10

ix. Caroline Israel (Source: KKBE Huguenin Avenue Cemetery.), born November 23, 1871; died

June 23, 1964 in Charleston, South Carolina; married Isaac S. Cohen; born March 31, 1871; died June 22, 1915 in Charleston, South Carolina.

More About Caroline Israel:
Cemetery: KKBE Huguenin Avenue

x. Edmund Israel (Source: Coming Street Cemetery.), born June 10, 1873; died September 21, 1877 in Charleston, South Carolina.

More About Edmund Israel:
Cemetery: Coming Street Cemetery

xi. Nathaniel Israel, born 1874; died 1959; married Estelle Rosenbaum; born 1885 in Philadelphia; died 1961.

Notes for Nathaniel Israel:
When Morris Israel died, he left his children a large inheritance. Nat was President of a bank called Charleston Savings. The bank went broke. Bailed out by the the family.

21 xii. Adelaide Israel, born November 04, 1876 in Charleston, South Carolina; died October 05, 1960 in Charleston , SC; married Montague Triest November 08, 1898 in Charleston, SC Married at home. by revised. B.A. Elzas. **The News & Courier**, 11/15/98.

xiii. Lee Clarence Israel, born 1879; died 1927; married Blanche Hirsch; born 1888; died 1957.

44. Herman Neuberger He married **45.**

Miriam.
   45. Miriam

Children of Herman Neuberger and Miriam are:
   22 i.   Max H. Neuberger, born May 27, 1878 in Savannah, Georgia; died July 20, 1906 in Tybee Beach, Savannah, Georgia; married Rosina Levy October 30, 1904 in Augusta, Georgia.
      ii.   Louie Neuberger
      iii. Fannie Neuberger

   46.   Jacob H. Levy (Source: (1) Magnolia Cemetery. Tombstone, (2) Malcolm H. Stern, **First American Jewish Families - 600 Genealogies - 1654 - 1988**, (Ottenheimer Publishers; 3rd ed. updated and revised edition (1988)), 167.), born November 23, 1858 in Augusta, Georgia; died May 09, 1919 in Augusta, GA (Source: Magnolia Cemetery.). He was the son of **92. A Levy** and **93. Rosina Henricks**. He married **47. Annie Brown** 1877.
   47.   Annie Brown (Source: (1) Magnolia Cemetery. Tombstone, (2) Malcolm H. Stern, **First American Jewish Families - 600 Genealogies - 1654 - 1988**, (Ottenheimer Publishers; 3rd ed. updated and revised edition (1988)), 167.), born January 12, 1860 in New York City, New York; died January 16, 1940 in Augusta, Georgia (Source: Magnolia Cemetery.). She was the daughter of **94. Simon Brown** and **95. Phillapena Brown**.

More About Jacob H. Levy:
Cemetery: May 10, 1919, Magnolia Cemetery, Augusta, GA, Walton Way Temple, Children of Israel

More About Annie Brown:
Cemetery: January 17, 1940, Magnolia Cemetery, Augusta, GA, Walton Way Temple, Children of Israel

More About Jacob Levy and Annie Brown:
Marriage: 1877

Children of Jacob Levy and Annie Brown are:
    i.   Issac S. Levy (Source: Malcolm H. Stern, **First American Jewish Families - 600 Genealogies - 1654 - 1988**, (Ottenheimer Publishers; 3rd ed. updated and revised edition (1988)), 167.), born January 1878 in South Carolina; died 1962 in Tampa, Florida; married Fannie Neuberger.
    ii.   Abram Levy (Source: (1) Malcolm H. Stern, **First American Jewish Families - 600 Genealogies - 1654 - 1988**, (Ottenheimer Publishers; 3rd Ed. updated and revised edition (1988)), 167., (2) Magnolia Cemetery. Tombstone), born September 24, 1880 in South Carolina; died March 27, 1932 in Augusta, GA; married Ina May Weil.

More About Abram Levy:
Cemetery: March 28, 1932, Augusta, GA, Magnolia Cemetery, Walton Way Temple, Children of Israel

    iii.   Pena Levy (Source: (1) James William Hagy, **This Happy Land - The Jews of Colonial and Antebellum Charleston**, (The University of Alabama Press 1993), 352., (2) Barnett Elzas, **The Jews of South Carolina, from the Earliest Times to the Present Day** , (Copyright 1905. First Edition), 129,136,278., (3) Malcolm H. Stern, **First American Jewish Families - 600 Genealogies -**

1654 - 1988, (Ottenheimer Publishers; 3rd Ed. updated and revised edition (1988)), 167.), born 1882 in South Carolina; died 1909; married Jacue Hirschi.

23 iv. Rosina Levy, born September 05, 1884 in Blackville, South Carolina; died August 12, 1972 in Charleston , SC; married (1) Max H. Neuberger October 30, 1904 in Augusta, Georgia; married (2) Simon Sorentrue, Sr. June 05, 1910 in Augusta, Georgia by Rabbi Barnett A. Elzas.

v. Essie Levy (Source: (1) Malcolm H. Stern, **First American Jewish Families - 600 Genealogies - 1654 - 1988**, (Ottenheimer Publishers; 3rd ed. updated and revised edition (1988)), 167., (2) Magnolia Cemetery. Tombstone), born September 03, 1886; died September 09, 1979 in Augusta, GA, Magnolia Cemetery, Walton Way Temple, Children of Israel; married Benedict S. Goldberg; born September 17, 1883; died March 11, 1970 in Augusta, GA, Magnolia Cemetery, Walton Way Temple, Children of Israel.

More About Essie Levy:
Cemetery: September 10, 1979, Magnolia Cemetery, Augusta, GA, Walton Way Temple, Children of Israel

More About Benedict S. Goldberg:
Cemetery: March 12, 1970, Magnolia Cemetery, Augusta, GA, Walton Way Temple, Children of Israel

60. David Esserman, born in Rome, Georgia; died in Rome, Georgia.

More About David Esserman:
Stone: 1st Rabbi in Rome, GA

Child of David Esserman is:

30 i. Joseph Esserman, born 1872; died May 27, 1927 in Rome, Georgia; married Fannie Mendelson.

Generation No. 7

64. Heineman Freudenberg, born in Freudenberg, Germany; died in Sittlinghause, Germany.

Children of Heineman Freudenberg are:
      i. Simon Freudenberg, born 1800 in Germany, Boedefeld; married Rahel Vogelsang; born 1804.
      ii. Mayer Freudenberg, born 1802.
      iii. Menke Freudenberg, born 1804.
      iv. Brendel Freudenberg, born 1806.
      v. Malchen Freudenberg, born 1810.
      vi. Issak Freudenberg, born 1812.
32 vii. Abraham Freudenberg, born 1818 in Germany, Boedefeld; died November 14, 1863; married (2) Unknown First Name Weil in Soestberg, Germany.

70. Leser Fischbein, born 1775; died May 03, 1868. He married **71. Sophie Vogelsang**.
71. Sophie Vogelsang, born December 26, 1796; died October 12, 1876.

Children of Leser Fischbein and Sophie Vogelsang are:

i. Bernard Fischbein, born February 04, 1818.

ii. Abraham Fischbein, born January 02, 1820.

35 iii. Helene Fischbein, born November 29, 1820 in Essen, Germany; died June 10, 1900; married Simon Buschoff.

iv. Pauline Fischbein, born November 13, 1823.

v. Calmon Fischbein, born May 18, 1825.

vi. Henriette Fischbein, born October 29, 1829.

vii. Levy Fischbein, born July 17, 1832.

viii. Johanna Fischbein, born September 17, 1835.

ix. Sophie Fischbein, born March 31, 1837.

x. Phillip Fischbein, born April 19, 1839.

xi. Rika Fischbein, born June 18, 1841.

xii. Hermann Fischbein, born January 23, 1844.

76. Leser Ganz, born 1822 in Bunde, Westphalia, Germany; died 1901. He married **77. Eva Levisohn**.

77. Eva Levisohn, born 1823 in Bunde, Westphalia, Germany; died 1919.

Child of Leser Ganz and Eva Levisohn is:

38 i. Alex Ganz, born 1848 in Bunde, Westphalia, Germany; died 1921 in Hanover, Germany; married Berta Stern.

78. Aaron Stern, born 1811. He married **79.**

Emile Loewenbach.

79. **Emile Loewenbach,** born 1815 in Niedermarsberg, Germany. She was the daughter of **158. Jacob Loewenbach.**

Child of Aaron Stern and Emile Loewenbach is:

39 i. Berta Stern, born 1860 in Geseke, Germany; died 1934 in Hanover, Germany; married Alex Ganz.

80. **Joseph Triest** (Source: Coming Street Cemetery.), born June 01, 1810 in Germany, Kingdom of Bavaria; died March 26, 1891 in Charleston , SC (Source: Barnett Elzas, **The Old Jewish Cemeteries at Charleston, SC,** (The Daggett Printing Company 1903).). He married **81. Caroline Hollander.**

81. **Caroline Hollander** (Source: (1) Barnett Elzas, **The Old Jewish Cemeteries at Charleston, SC,** (The Daggett Printing Company 1903)., (2) Coming Street Cemetery.), born January 09, 1808; died November 01, 1878 in Charleston , SC (Source: Barnett Elzas, **The Old Jewish Cemeteries at Charleston, SC,** (The Daggett Printing Company 1903).).

More About Joseph Triest:
Cemetery: March 26, 1891, Coming Street Cemetery
Stone: March 26, 1891, "May his soul rest in peace" on her stone at Coming Street

More About Caroline Hollander:
Cemetery: November 01, 1878, Coming Street Cemetery

Stone: November 01, 1878, "May her soul rest in peace" on her stone at Coming Street

Child of Joseph Triest and Caroline Hollander is:
40 i. Maier Triest, born August 09, 1831 in Germany, Kingdom of Bavaria; died August 18, 1894 in Charleston , SC; married Hannah Reichman February 10, 1869 in Ohio, Cincinnati.

82. Raphael Reichman, born 1823 in Germany. He married **83. Frances**
83. Frances, born 1822 in Germany.

More About Raphael Reichman:
Merchant: 1870 US Census
Occupation: Merchant/Tailor
Residence: 1870, Milwaukee, WI

Children of Raphael Reichman and Frances are:
41 i. Hannah Reichman, born 1849 in Bookenheim, Germany; died September 02, 1929 in New York City, New York; married Maier Triest February 10, 1869 in Ohio, Cincinnati.
ii. Pauline Reichman, born 1853.
iii. John Reichman

86. Levy Elias (Source: (1) Malcolm Stern, First Families, (2) James William Hagy, **This Happy Land - The Jews of Colonial and Antebellum Charleston,** (The University of Alabama Press 1993), 314.), born 1800 in Dedesdorf, Germany; died December 30, 1877 in Columbia, South Carolina (Source: "Charleston News & Courier," Obituary.).

He married **87. Rosa Lilienthal.**

87. Rosa Lilienthal (Source: (1) James William Hagy, **This Happy Land - The Jews of Colonial and Antebellum Charleston,** (The University of Alabama Press 1993), (2) Malcolm H. Stern, **First American Jewish Families - 600 Genealogies - 1654 - 1988,** (Ottenheimer Publishers; 3rd ed. updated and revised edition (1988)), 63.).

Notes for Levy Elias:
Elias--Died, in this city, December 30th, 1877, Mr. Levy Elias, in the seventy-seventh year of his age.

The subject of this obituary was born in Dedesdorf, Germany, in the year 1800, and for almost half a century resided in this State, his adopted home, where he enjoyed the felicity of rearing a large family, who, with their offspring, constituted the chief happiness of his life. His death has left the impress of woe upon many stricken hearts, to which he was a source of comfort and pleasure.

Genial and kind-hearted in disposition, his soul was ever instinct with heavenly impulses of Charity, not mere almsgiving, but lavishly manifested in those higher and holier offices to the sick, the dying and the dead. In these benevolent ministrations his sympathies were always active, and he delighted in opportunities of affording relief.

He bore his protracted illness with meekness and resignation, never darkening the brightness of his faith with a single murmur. With unwavering confidence in his Creator he calmly awaited His summons, and without a struggle his spirit departed to a purer and a better world.

The News & Courier. January 5, 1878.

More About Levy Elias:
Residence: 1830, First Recorded year in SC. Stern.

68

Notes for Rosa Lilienthal:
Per Adelaide T. Jacobs, the Lilienthals are from Selma, Alabama. Also check Threefoot family for a connection with Lilienthal.

Children of Levy Elias and Rosa Lilienthal are:

43 i. Rebecca Elias, born October 16, 1839 in St. Augustine, Florida; died December 05, 1896 in Charleston , SC; married Morris Israel August 10, 1859 in Abbyville, SC.

ii. Lewis Elias (Source: (1) James William Hagy, **This Happy Land - The Jews of Colonial and Antebellum Charleston,** (The University of Alabama Press 1993), 63., (2) Malcolm H. Stern, **First American Jewish Families - 600 Genealogies - 1654 - 1988,** (Ottenheimer Publishers; 3rd ed. updated and revised edition (1988)), 63., (3) KKBE Huguenin Avenue Cemetery.), born January 10, 1840; died October 15, 1916 in Charleston, South Carolina; married Marian; born February 02, 1842; died April 23, 1913 in Charleston, South Carolina.

More About Lewis Elias:
Cemetery: October 15, 1916, KKBE Huguenin Avenue

More About Marian:
Cemetery: April 23, 1913, KKBE Huguenin Avenue

iii. Mary Ann Elias

Notes for Mary Ann Elias:
Check Coming Street Cemetery

iv. Esther Elias, married Ned Spanier.

92. A Levy (Source: (1) Malcolm H. Stern, **First American Jewish Families - 600 Genealogies - 1654 - 1988,** (Ottenheimer Publishers; 3rd ed. updated and revised edition (1988)), 167., (2) Magnolia Cemetery. Tombstone)**,** born 1820 in Hamburg, SC; died September 03, 1879 in Augusta, GA (Source: Magnolia Cemetery.). He was the son of **184. Nathan Levy** and **185. Sarah Unknown**. He married **93. Rosina Henricks**.

93. Rosina Henricks (Source: Malcolm H. Stern, **First American Jewish Families - 600 Genealogies - 1654 - 1988,** (Ottenheimer Publishers; 3rd ed. updated and revised edition (1988)), 167.)**,** born January 1829; died February 1888. She was the daughter of **186. Isaac Henricks** and **187. Esther Phillips**.

More About A Levy:
Cemetery: September 04, 1879, Augusta, GA, Magnolia Cemetery, Walton Way Temple, Children of Israel

Children of A Levy and Rosina Henricks are:
i. I. Clarence Levy (Source: (1) Malcolm H. Stern, **First American Jewish Families - 600 Genealogies - 1654 - 1988,** (Ottenheimer Publishers; 3rd ed. updated and revised edition (1988)), 167., (2) Magnolia Cemetery. Tombstone), born January 12, 1850 in Hamburg, SC; died September 23, 1897 in Augusta, GA; married Ida Brady February 25, 1874; born December 15, 1855 in Charleston, South

70

Carolina; died January 15, 1938 in Augusta, GA.

More About I. Clarence Levy:
Cemetery: September 24, 1897, Augusta, GA, Magnolia Cemetery, Walton Way Temple, Children of Israel

More About Ida Brady:
Cemetery: January 16, 1938, Augusta, GA, Magnolia Cemetery, Walton Way Temple, Children of Israel

More About I. Levy and Ida Brady:
Marriage: February 25, 1874

    ii. Alice Levy (Source: Malcolm H. Stern, **First American Jewish Families - 600 Genealogies - 1654 - 1988**, (Ottenheimer Publishers; 3rd ed. updated and revised edition (1988)), 167.), born 1852 in Hamburg, SC; married Matthew Marcus.

46 iii. Jacob H. Levy, born November 23, 1858 in Augusta, Georgia; died May 09, 1919 in Augusta, GA; married Annie Brown 1877.

    iv. J. Willie Levy (Source: Malcolm H. Stern, **First American Jewish Families - 600 Genealogies - 1654 - 1988**, (Ottenheimer Publishers; 3rd ed. updated and revised edition (1988)), 167.), born December 1859 in Hamburg, SC; married Adelaide Solomon; born September 1864.

    v. Matilda Levy (Source: Malcolm H. Stern, **First American Jewish Families - 600 Genealogies - 1654 - 1988**, (Ottenheimer Publishers; 3rd ed. updated and revised edition (1988)), 167.), born 1866 in Augusta, Georgia.

    vi. Esther Levy (Source: Malcolm H. Stern, **First American Jewish Families - 600 Genealogies**

71

- **1654 - 1988**, (Ottenheimer Publishers; 3rd Ed. updated and revised edition (1988)), 167.), born 1868 in Augusta, Georgia.

vii. Ida Fannie Levy (Source: Magnolia Cemetery.), died in Augusta, GA.

More About Ida Fannie Levy:
Cemetery: Augusta, GA, Magnolia Cemetery, Walton Way Temple, Children of Israel
Stone: "Age 12 years, 10 months" at death

94. Simon Brown (Source: (1) Magnolia Cemetery. Tombstone, (2) Robert N. Rosen, **The Jewish Confederates**, (University of SC Press 2000), 202, Immigrants from German States. Lived in NY. Moved to SC to establish new life in Blackville, SC. Pena feared Simon's involvement with Russian anarchists. Simon was a reluctant confederate. Enlisted 7th SC April 1864. Captured August 1864.), born September 20, 1829 in Warsaw, Poland (Source: Magnolia Cemetery.); died December 05, 1906 in Blackville, South Carolina. He married **95. Phillapena Brown**.

95. Phillapena Brown (Source: (1) Magnolia Cemetery. Tombstone, (2) Robert N. Rosen, **The Jewish Confederates**, (University of SC Press 2000), 202, Immigrants from German States. Lived in NY. Moved to SC to establish new life in Blackville, SC. Pena feared Simon's involvement with Russian anarchists. Simon was a reluctant confederate. Enlisted 7th SC April 1864. Captured August 1864. .), born May 10, 1829 in Filehne, Germany (Source: Magnolia Cemetery.); died August 20, 1918.

More About Simon Brown:
Burial: December 06, 1906, Augusta, GA, Magnolia
Cemetery, Walton Way Temple, Children of Israel
Military service: 1864, Confederate Soldier

More About Phillapena Brown:
Cemetery: August 21, 1918, Augusta, GA, Magnolia
Cemetery, Walton Way Temple, Children of Israel

Child of Simon Brown and Phillapena Brown is:
   47 i.   Annie Brown, born January 12, 1860 in
New York City, New York; died January 16, 1940 in
Augusta, Georgia; married Jacob H. Levy 1877.

Generation No. 8

   158.   **Jacob   Loewenbach,**   born   1775   in
Niedermarsberg, Germany.

Child of Jacob Loewenbach is:
   79 i.   Emile   Loewenbach,   born   1815   in
Niedermarsberg, Germany; married Aaron Stern.

   184. Nathan Levy (Source: Malcolm H. Stern,
**First American Jewish Families - 600 Genealogies
- 1654 - 1988,**   (Ottenheimer Publishers; 3rd ed.
updated and revised edition (1988)), 167.)**,** born 1758
in Holland; died January 29, 1827 in Charleston,
South Carolina. He married **185. Sarah.**
   185.   Sarah (Source: Malcolm H. Stern, **First
American Jewish Families - 600 Genealogies -
1654 - 1988,**   (Ottenheimer Publishers; 3rd ed.
updated and revised edition (1988)), 167.)**,** born 1781

in England; died August 13, 1822 in Charleston, South Carolina.

Children of Nathan Levy and Sarah Unknown are:
      i.   Lewis Levy (Source: (1) James William Hagy, **This Happy Land - The Jews of Colonial and Antebellum Charleston,** (The University of Alabama Press 1993), 351., (2) Barnett Elzas, **The Jews of South Carolina, from the Earliest Times to the Present Day** , (Copyright 1905. First Edition), 231., (3) Malcolm H. Stern, **First American Jewish Families - 600 Genealogies - 1654 - 1988,** (Ottenheimer Publishers; 3rd ed. updated and revised edition (1988)), 167.), born 1802; died 1866.

More About Lewis Levy:
Residence: 1846, First recorded year in SC

      ii.   Moses Levy (Source: (1) James William Hagy, **This Happy Land - The Jews of Colonial and Antebellum Charleston,** (The University of Alabama Press 1993), 352., (2) Malcolm H. Stern, **First American Jewish Families - 600 Genealogies - 1654 - 1988,** (Ottenheimer Publishers; 3rd Ed. updated and revised edition (1988)), 167.), born February 19, 1803; died 1804.

More About Moses Levy:
Residence: 1804, First recorded year in SC

      AI.   Issac A. Levy (Source: (1) James William Hagy, **This Happy Land - The Jews of Colonial and Antebellum Charleston,** (The University of Alabama Press 1993), 347,350., (2) Malcolm H. Stern,

First American Jewish Families - 600 Genealogies - 1654 - 1988, (Ottenheimer Publishers; 3rd ed. updated and revised edition (1988)), 58,167.), born 1809 in Charleston , SC; died November 09, 1871 in Augusta, GA; married Angelique Heydenfeldt 1841.

More About Issac A. Levy:
Residence: 1809, First recorded year in SC
Role in KKBE Reforming: Bet. 1840 - 1843, Member of Sherith Israel

More About Issac Levy and Angelique Heydenfeldt:
Marriage: 1841

92 iv. A Levy, born 1820 in Hamburg, SC; died September 03, 1879 in Augusta, GA; married Rosina Henricks.

v. Samuel Levy (Source: (1) James William Hagy, **This Happy Land - The Jews of Colonial and Antebellum Charleston**, (The University of Alabama Press 1993), 353., (2) Malcolm H. Stern, **First American Jewish Families - 600 Genealogies - 1654 - 1988**, (Ottenheimer Publishers; 3rd ed. updated and revised edition (1988)), 167,247.), born 1821 in Oldenburg, Germany; died in Augusta, GA; married (1) Hannah Henricks; born October 24, 1824; married (2) Hannah Henricks October 24, 1845 in Hamburg, SC; born August 30, 1824 in Charleston, South Carolina; died December 19, 1893 in Augusta, GA.

More About Samuel Levy:
Burial: Augusta, GA, Magnolia Cemetery, Walton Way Temple, Children of Israel
Cemetery: Magnolia Cemetery, Augusta, GA, Walton

75

186. **Isaac Henricks** (Source: (1) Magnolia Cemetery., (2) Malcolm H. Stern, **First American Jewish Families - 600 Genealogies - 1654 - 1988,** (Ottenheimer Publishers; 3rd Ed. updated and revised edition (1988)), 247.)**,** born 1770 in Augusta, Georgia; died March 13, 1848 in Augusta, GA. He married **187. Esther Phillips**.

187. **Esther Phillips** (Source: (1) James William Hagy, **This Happy Land - The Jews of Colonial and Antebellum Charleston,** (The University of Alabama Press 1993), 327., (2) Malcolm H. Stern, **First American Jewish Families - 600 Genealogies - 1654 - 1988,** (Ottenheimer Publishers; 3rd ed. updated and revised edition (1988)), 247., (3) Magnolia Cemetery.)**,** born December 06, 1794; died January 23, 1883 in Augusta, GA. She was the daughter of **374. Jacob Phillps** and **375. Hannah Isaacks**.

More About Isaac Henricks:
Cemetery: March 14, 1848, Augusta, GA, Magnolia Cemetery, Walton Way Temple, Children of Israel (Source: Magnolia Cemetery, Tombstone.)
Stone: 1854, Died in a duel

More About Esther Phillips:
Cemetery: January 24, 1883, Augusta, GA, Magnolia Cemetery, Walton Way Temple, Children of Israel (Source: Magnolia Cemetery Tombstone)

Children of Isaac Henricks and Esther Phillips are:
　　93　i.　Rosina Henricks, born January 1829; died

February 1888; married A Levy.

    ii.   Hannah Henricks, born October 24, 1824; married Samuel Levy; born 1821 in Oldenburg, Germany; died in Augusta, GA.

More About Samuel Levy:
Burial: Augusta, GA, Magnolia Cemetery, Walton Way Temple, Children of Israel
Cemetery: Magnolia Cemetery, Augusta, GA, Walton Way Temple, Children of Israel

    iii.   Jacob Henricks, born 1825; died 1857.
    iv.   Henry Henricks, born 1826; died in New Orleans.
    v.   Abraham Isaacs Henricks, born 1827; died in Texas; married Rachel Sampson; died in Texas.
    vi.   Benjamin Franklin Henricks, born 1828 in Augusta, GA; died December 1910 in Austin, Texas; married (1) Frances Solomons August 21, 1859 in Rome, Georgia; born July 1827; died October 06, 1866 in Austin, Texas; married (2) Frances Levine 1869 in Texas.

More About Benjamin Henricks and Frances Solomons:
Marriage: August 21, 1859, Rome, Georgia

Generation No. 9

    374.   Jacob Phillips (Source: Submitted by Dorothy Ida Morse née Levy, *Application for Membership to The National Society of the Daughters of the American Revolution,* (Application approved January 31, 1928), National Number 238769.), born 1750 in

England; died 1820 in Charleston, South Carolina. He married **375. Hannah Isaacks** August 13, 1785 in Newport, RI.

375. Hannah Isaacks (Source: (1) James William Hagy, **This Happy Land - The Jews of Colonial and Antebellum Charleston,** (The University of Alabama Press 1993), 388., (2) Malcolm H. Stern, **First American Jewish Families - 600 Genealogies - 1654 - 1988,** (Ottenheimer Publishers; 3rd ed. updated and revised edition (1988)), 120., (3) Henry Aaron Alexander, *Notes on The Alexander Family of South Carolina and Georgia and Connections - 1651-1954,* (1954)., (4) Malcolm H. Stern, **First American Jewish Families - 600 Genealogies - 1654 - 1988,** (Ottenheimer Publishers; 3rd ed. updated and revised edition (1988)), 120,247.), born in Newport, RI or Jamaica; died March 08, 1798 in Martinique. She was the daughter of **750. Jacob Isaacks** and **751. Rebecca Mears**.

More About Jacob Phillips:
Military service: 1781, Revolutionary War Veteren
Residence: 1780, First recorded year in SC

More About Jacob Phillips and Hannah Isaacks:
Marriage: August 13, 1785, Newport, RI

Children of Jacob Phillips and Hannah Isaacks are:
      i. Rachel Phillips (Source: Malcolm H. Stern, **First American Jewish Families - 600 Genealogies - 1654 - 1988,** (Ottenheimer Publishers; 3rd Ed. updated and revised edition (1988)), 247.), born October 05, 1786 in Newport, RI; died October 05, 1870; married Michael Myers October 10, 1802; born October 25, 1763 in Sussex, England; died 1828.

More About Michael Myers:
Residence: 1800, First recorded year in SC

More About Michael Myers and Rachel Phillips:
Marriage: October 10, 1802

    ii. Abraham Phillips (Source: (1) James William Hagy, **This Happy Land - The Jews of Colonial and Antebellum Charleston,** (The University of Alabama Press 1993), 388., (2) Malcolm H. Stern, **First American Jewish Families - 600 Genealogies - 1654 - 1988,** (Ottenheimer Publishers; 3rd ed. updated and revised edition (1988)), 247., (3) Barnett Elzas, **The Jews of South Carolina, from the Earliest Times to the Present Day** , (Copyright 1905. First Edition), 138., (4) Coming Street Cemetery., (5) War of 1812 Veteran.), born March 24, 1788 in New York City, New York; died April 15, 1813 in Drowned off Norfolk, VA.

More About Abraham Phillips:
Burial: 1813, Drowned off Norfolk. War of 1812, Midshipman in the USN
Cause of Death: Drowned
Military service: 1813, War of 1812
Residence: 1809, First recorded year in SC

    iii. Frances Phillips (Source: (1) James William Hagy, **This Happy Land - The Jews of Colonial and Antebellum Charleston,** (The University of Alabama Press 1993), 319., (2) Malcolm H. Stern, **First American Jewish Families - 600 Genealogies - 1654 - 1988,** (Ottenheimer Publishers; 3rd Ed. updated and revised edition (1988)), 247., (3)

79

Coming Street Cemetery.), born February 05, 1790; died March 04, 1848 in Charleston , SC; married Isaac M. Goldsmith; born 1774; died September 26, 1821 in Charleston, South Carolina.

More About Frances Phillips:
Cemetery: May 04, 1848, Coming Street Cemetery
Residence: 1835, First recorded year in SC
Stone: May 04, 1848, Consort of the late Isaac Goldsmith

More About Isaac M. Goldsmith:
Residence: 1803, First recorded year in SC

iv. Rebecca Phillips (Source: (1) James William Hagy, **This Happy Land - The Jews of Colonial and Antebellum Charleston**, (The University of Alabama Press 1993), 377., (2) Malcolm H. Stern, **First American Jewish Families - 600 Genealogies - 1654 - 1988**, (Ottenheimer Publishers; 3rd ed. updated and revised edition (1988)), 120,247., (3) Theodore and Dale Rosengarten, **A Portion of the People - Three Hundred Years of Southern Jewish Life**, (University of SC Press 2000), 101., (4) Judith Shanks, Rebecca Isiah Moses by Rebecca's great-great-great-granddaughter.), born March 19, 1792 in Atlantic Ocean, At Sea; died December 24, 1872; married Isaiah Moses November 11, 1807; born 1772; died 1857.

Notes for Rebecca Phillips:
Biographical Notes on Rebecca Phillips Moses

Rebecca's birth was recorded by her father, Jacob Phillips: "My dear daughter Rebecca was born March

19, 1792." The words were written in Phillips's Haftarah, a collection of holy writings read in Jewish services. Jacob Phillips had emigrated from England to St. Eustatius as a youth, and then, in 1780, still young, to South Carolina, where he joined the militia to fight with the Patriots in the American Revolution.

Jacob Phillips traveled the Atlantic seaboard as a cargo merchant. His work took him as far north as Newport, Rhode Island, and down to New York, Charleston, and the West Indies. His wife, Hannah Isaacks--her family also in trade and shipping--lived in Newport until a business decline during the Revolutionary War prompted a family move to New York. Hannah's parents, Jacob and Rebecca Mears Isaacks, returned to Newport after the Revolution.

Hannah, Jacob, and their children lived at times in New York, Rhode Island, Saint Eustatius (in the West Indies), and South Carolina. Hannah sometimes traveled with Jacob to visit family along his route.

Because of this mobility, and because Jacob Phillips did not note the location of Rebecca's birth, we do not know where she was born. Family historians agree on the West Indies, but they disagree as to precisely where. One story puts Rebecca's birth at sea, a version of events picked up by Jewish genealogist Malcolm Stern. South Carolina historian James Hagy, in enumerating the origins of the Jews of South Carolina, reiterates this in his listing "born at sea," one person.

Giving birth at sea seems very unusual today. But in the late 18th and early 19th centuries, hundreds of children were raised on board ship, and many of them were born at sea. One ship captain delivered all six of his children.

According to family lore, Rebecca might have been born on Martinique (her mother died there six years later), St. Eustatius then known as St. Statia, (her parents lived there before her birth), Jamaica (some of her mother's family lived there), or St. Thomas.

Rebecca was named for her maternal grandmother, Rebecca Mears Isaacks, who was still alive when Rebecca was born. Although Jews following Ashkenazic (German) ritual would not name a baby for a living relative, the practice of naming a child after a living relative was part of the Sephardic tradition and was widely followed at the time, especially in the Americas, even among Jews of Ashkenazic origin.

The year 1798 was difficult for Rebecca Mears Isaacks. Several close family members died: her husband, Jacob Isaacks, who had been ill for a long time; her daughter Hannah, who left six young children; and her husband's brother Moses Isaacks, who was also the husband of her sister Judith Rachel. (Moses and Rachel Isaacks may not have lived in S.C. at the time, but several of their children did.)

Rebecca Isaacks soon moved with her living, unmarried children and grandchildren to Charleston. Rebecca Isaacks was 60; her granddaughter Rebecca was six.

Rebecca Isaacks died at age 64 in 1802, four years

after she had moved to Charleston. Ages of the Phillips children at the time ranged from 16 (Rachel) to six (Philip). Young Rebecca was 10. (Rebecca Isaacks's unmarried daughter, Rachel Isaacks, died soon after at age 22 in the small village of Cheraw, S.C.)

These nuggets of information evoke a picture in which the young children lived and visited with various cousins and family friends in Charleston and in Cheraw.

According to family historian Hannah Marie Moses, Rebecca was adopted by Sally Lopez, who taught her housekeeping skills and about her Jewish religion. The Lopez family was descended from Aaron Lopez, a Newport merchant. Aaron Lopez had been quite successful before the Revolution, but he lost ships during the war and consequently his fortune; some of his family afterwards relocated to S.C. (Sally Lopez's niece, also named Sally Lopez, organized religious education for children at Charleston's Kahal Kadosh Beth Elohim (KKBE) Congregation in 1838.)

More about Isaiah Moses:
ISAIAH & Rebecca MOSES: Merchant, Planter, Traditional Jew

When Isaiah Moses arrived in America from Europe around 1800, he came to Charleston, a thriving port city. Few details are known about his personal or family life before then. He was born in 1772. Originally from Bederkese, Hanover, he first moved to England in the early 1790s, where he married a woman whose identity is now unknown and with

83

whom he had four sons in the 1790s.

When his wife died, likely in childbirth, he moved to Charleston, S.C. Probably he left his sons in England. However, at least one of his sons was in Charleston in 1804 and was a member of KKBE three years before Isaiah married Rebecca. These sons, Phineas, Morris, Solomon, and Simeon Moses would be among the first Jews to settle in Cincinnati.

Isaiah was doubtless aware of Charleston as a thriving Jewish center: Of the 140 Jewish men new to Charleston's KKBE congregation between 1776 and 1825, one-third came from England although like Isaiah Moses, many were born elsewhere. For the first two decades of the 19th century, the Jewish population of Charleston exceeded that of any other U.S. city. Hagy estimates the number of Jews in Charleston at 600 in the year 1800.

In pre-Revolutionary times, Charleston's reputation as a prosperous town was based on the profitability of indigo. The crop had ceased being profitable when the "bounty" offered for it by the British was no longer available. The low country on the Carolina coast around Charleston was also under rice cultivation, another profitable crop that had made many planters wealthy. But rice was not invariably profitable, as Isaiah would one day discover.

Isaiah Moses's presence in Charleston is first documented in the Charleston city directory of 1800. His early years there were a financial success, probably the most so of his career. Isaiah's first listing is as a grocer, a provisioner for the plantation owners who would come to town. Subsequent listings indicate he was a shopkeeper, then planter.

The distinctions between "shopkeeper" and "merchant" may not be obvious to us today. A merchant bought and sold on his own account and tried to find a market for what he purchased. A shopkeeper had a fixed place of business from which he served retail customers. The social hierarchy of the time placed merchants higher on the socioeconomic scale than shopkeepers; Isaiah was a merchant, according to historian James Hagy. Planters were considered the professional and social elite, and Isaiah early on had ambitions in this area. (In Bederkese, Hanover, where he was born, Jews had not been permitted even to own land.)

Providing for himself and perhaps sending money home for four children may have motivated his move to America. Through the closeness of the Jewish community and his strong religious ties, Isaiah Moses met Rebecca Phillips, a young woman of 15. Isaiah was doing well in business; he was a respected, responsible member of the Jewish community, and thereby a likely prospect for the young Rebecca. His years in England, as for many Ashkenazic Jews, provided a bridge from his youth in Hanover to his mature adulthood in Charleston, Anglicizing him in the process. It was probably in England that he first became exposed to the Sephardic ritual that he so staunchly upheld in South Carolina.

R.I. MOSES: Life as a Wife, Mother, and Businesswoman

85

Rebecca and Isaiah married on November 11, 1807. Rebecca had a ketubah, or Jewish marriage contract, worked out earlier. Another traditional Jewish document related to her marriage was a shetar halitzah, signed at the time of her wedding. The prenuptial shetar halitzah, signed by Levi Moses, Isaiah's brother, freed her from the obligation of a Levirate marriage, that is, marrying Isaiah's brother Levi if Isaiah should die before Rebecca had children.

The wedding was in Charleston and took place on Wednesday, a traditional wedding day for young Jewish brides at the time; weddings were usually held at home. The only known description of a Jewish wedding in early America was written by Dr. Benjamin Rush in a letter to his wife, and he spoke of elements retained today in traditional Orthodox Jewish weddings. (Later, in 1841, the congregation asked the female members to furnish a white chuppah, or wedding canopy, for congregational use in the synagogue.)

When Rebecca married Isaiah, she was aged 15 years, eight months, and he was 35. Though this was young for a Jewish bride in Charleston in the early 19th century, five years younger than average, a 20- year difference in ages between husband and wife, though not the norm, was also not unusual at the time. Rebecca's older sister Rachel at 17 had married a man 23 years older than she. Her grandmother had married a man 20 years older. Later, Rebecca's younger sister Fanny married a man 16 years older than she. Isaiah's brother Levi, who had come to South Carolina with Isaiah, also married a woman who was about 16 at the time of the marriage.

86

By 1807, Rebecca's mother had been dead for 10 years. Her grandmother, who had helped raise her, had been dead for five years. Her father's business as a seagoing merchant kept him traveling along the eastern seaboard. Her young aunt Rachel Phillips had recently died at age 22, perhaps of one of the fevers that periodically raged in South Carolina. So many deaths and so much change in her short life may have made Isaiah Moses a safe haven for her.

Regardless of such influences on her decision to marry, glimpses into her daybook of later years reveal Rebecca to have been a practical woman, and she doubtless welcomed the opportunity to marry. In a brief daybook entry upon Isaiah's death 50 years later, she refers to him as her "beloved husband." No doubt he was.

Rebecca dropped her maiden name, Phillips, and took her husband's given name as her middle name. She is listed in the city directory of 1837 as "Moses, R. I.," and she also uses this initial on the cover of her daybook. Isaiah also gave his name to each of his sons as a middle name. At the time Isaiah was born in Germany, a son's second name was the name of his father. Thus Isaiah Moses was Isaiah, son of Moses. (The Isaiah Moses Jr. first listed in Charleston in 1804 by historian James Hagy, would have been a son by his first wife.)

Rebecca gave birth to her first child a year after her marriage. Though Isaiah continued his business in Charleston after the marriage, her first three children were born in Columbia, according to notations in a family bible.

Who or what provided the draw for Rebecca away from Charleston for her first three confinements remains a mystery, but it was traditional to go back to a parental home to give birth. According to a family history, Rebecca's own daughter Cecilia returned to her parents' (Rebecca and Isaiah's) home in Charleston to give birth to her daughter Rebecca Ella Solomons. And Rebecca's older sister had been born at her grandparents' in Newport, Rhode Island.

Another possibility is that Isaiah was attracted to Columbia by the lots being auctioned for sale. However, he continues to be listed in Charleston directories of this period.

In 1813, Rebecca bore her fourth child--this time in Charleston. With the purchase that year of the Oaks plantation on Goose Creek, Rebecca and Isaiah settled more solidly into Charleston and the low country, as the coastal area around Charleston is called. Her father, Jacob Phillips, at some point moved into Rebecca and Isaiah's home. By then he was crippled from rheumatism, said to have resulted from his many years at sea. He was bedridden during his last years in Rebecca's home; he died around 1830.

Isaiah was able to buy the Oaks because of his success in business. He also bought 35 slaves to work the plantation. With this symbol of a wealthy southern man, he began to be listed in the city directory as "planter." No doubt Isaiah expected to make money from the plantation, but in this he was disappointed.

An 1819 plat of the plantation shows the land around the creek under cultivation for rice, which had a reputation as a profitable crop in the low country. But Isaiah Moses had at most a few dozen acres under rice cultivation, far fewer than the hundred acres necessary to justify the expense of tidal irrigation.

The Charleston area went into economic decline in the late eighteen-teens through the early eighteen-twenties. There are several reasons for this, including the end of the prosperous post-Revolutionary War economy; the publicized slave revolt of Denmark Vesey in 1822, which scared many whites away. Regular steamship service between Europe and New York and Philadelphia diminished the importance of Charleston and its favorable location along the Atlantic jet stream flowing from the West Indies to Europe. Competition from other Southern ports attracting more trade contributed to Charleston's decline.

Wide-scale economic depression in 1837 strained Isaiah's income further. In this one year only, Rebecca Moses is listed in the Charleston directory as having a dry-goods business.

To tide them over through the tough time, Isaiah borrowed $2,000 from the general endowment fund of the synagogue, which was available for personal loans. Then the plantation house burned down in 1840. Isaiah sold the Oaks property in 1841 at a $2,000 loss from the original purchase price of $6,000.

In addition to his business interests--which at one point included a partnership in an auction business-- Isaiah was actively involved in the Charleston Jewish community. Probably his early success as a grocer and merchant/shopkeeper enabled him to become a financial supporter and leader of the Esnoga, as the place of worship was called according to Sephardic custom. At the time of the 1820 adoption of the constitution of KKBE Congregation, Isaiah Moses served on the Adjuncta, or governing board. Although he came from Germany, Isaiah was a strong proponent of the traditional Sephardic ritual, and he opposed the reforms generally supported by the German Jews of the Congregation.

Isaiah Moses was a supporter and leader of the breakaway Shearit Israel congregation after his original congregation, KKBE, became Reform. His son-in-law, revised. Jacob Rosenfeld, was the hassan-- the cantor or reader--of the congregation. Isaiah was also a member of the Hebrew Orphan Society, of which his son Levy was president immediately before the Civil War.

The Charleston city directories of the period provide glimpses into social history. Most listings are for businesses, but some are residential. Typically, in early-19th-century Charleston, residences were above businesses, in the same building. The family living above the business may have been the one running the business, but not necessarily. Between 1800 and 1849, Isaiah Moses is listed in the city directories at various addresses, mostly on King Street. Only from 1802 to 1807 is he listed at the same address, 197 King Street. He later bought a building on King

Street, but it is not known whether this was used as a residence, a business address, or an investment-- probably in each capacity at various times. There was one listing on St. Phillips Street. One family history, written by Rebecca Moses's great-grandson H. A. Alexander, says that his mother, Rebecca Ella Solomons Alexander, "was born in 1854 in the same house in the same bed in which her mother (Cecilia Moses Solomons) was born." The listings apparently are collected by the company printing the directory and appear not to be consistently inclusive but rather indicative.

Wherever the family lived, it was probably within walking distance of the Esnoga. As traditionally observant Jews, the family would have walked to services on the sabbath and other holidays.

Like other plantation owners, the Moseses spent the hottest months away from the plantation, probably in town, and in fact it is not clear how much time the family spent at the plantation. Though the plantation was located within 20 miles of Charleston, it would have taken the better part of a day to get there by carriage. With Isaiah's active role in the Esnoga, the family likely spent more time in town than on the farm for religious holidays and a majority of weekly sabbaths.

Rebecca stayed busy with her large and growing family. Her health as a child-bearing woman is remarkable: All 12 of her children were born in good health, and her own health was not jeopardized. Rebecca's children were born starting when she was 16 and Isaiah 36, her last child when she was 41 and

Isaiah 61.

Her young children appear to have been healthy, although her son Moses suffered from dementia as an adult. In her daybook Rebecca refers to his living at Columbia Insane Asylum beginning in 1845, when he was 27; he died 18 years later. He seemed to be the only child whose welfare she felt the need to provide for after her death. She stipulated in her will that if Moses were still alive when she died, she wanted her house to go for his care. Moses in fact died in 1863, at age 45, nine years before Rebecca's death.

Contrasting with her good health were the health-related early deaths of her mother, at age 36; her cousin Rachel Isaacks, at age 22; and her husband's first wife. Of her daughters' children, several died as infants, including those of Sarah, Cecilia, and Leonora.

Rebecca and Isaiah's close-knit family developed strong ties to other families through multiple marriages to the same family--across several generations--a common practice among early American Jews, documented by Jewish genealogist Malcolm Stern and others. In Rebecca's family it is striking: As already noted, Rebecca's grandmother and a sister had married two brothers. Son Jacob Moses married Rinah J. Ottolengui, and then nine years later—after Rinah had died—married her sister Sarah Ottolengui. Son Aaron married another Ottolengui sister, Judith A. Offspring from each of these marriages wed in the next generation. Another Moses daughter, Cecilia, married a first cousin of the Ottolengui women (Abraham Alexander Solomons).

Some of these family alliances took place over several generations. One of Cecilia's children, Rebecca Ella Solomons, married Julius M. Alexander, the son of another of Rebecca's daughters, Sarah Moses Alexander, and her husband, Aaron Alexander. Offspring of Isaiah Moses's son of his first wife married offspring descended from children with his second wife, Rebecca. There were also multiple marriages across several generations with the Joseph, Solomons, and Abrahams families.

Rebecca noted in her daybook several visits to her daughters' homes. Her daughter Leonora and husband revised. Jacob Rosenfeld lived for a time in Cincinnati, where Isaiah Moses's sons had been instrumental in founding an early congregation, and in Savannah, where son-in-law Abraham Alexander Solomons, married to Cecilia Moses Solomons, was active in the politics of Congregation Mickve Israel and was instrumental in hiring Rosenfeld as its rabbi. Rebecca does not mention any of Isaiah's children with his first wife in her daybook, but the marriages among descendants of both unions suggest the families stayed in touch.

Several of Rebecca's children were active in their congregations. Her sons remained aligned with Isaiah in their choice of a traditional congregation. Rebecca's daughters were involved in religious education. Leonora taught children alongside her husband, and Sarah Moses Alexander taught children in her home in Atlanta. There is no evidence that Rebecca herself formally instructed children.

In political matters, especially regarding slavery and the South, there was not consistent agreement in the family. During the Civil War, one of Rebecca's daughters, Sarah, along with her husband, Aaron Alexander, staunchly supported the Union, whereas Rebecca just as strongly supported the Southern cause. Aaron and Sarah had moved from Charleston to Atlanta, but sometime in the 1850s, they moved with their family to Philadelphia. This period was financially devastating to them, and he ended up in debtors prison; Sarah followed him into prison with their children. The family moved to Georia during the war and back Atlanta after the war; Aaron became financially successful in Atlanta. In the tradition of a number of Charleston-born Jews of the period, both Aaron and Sarah were buried in the old Coming Street cemetery in Charleston.

A story revealing Rebecca's practical side is charmingly recounted by Hannah Marie Moses, a granddaughter, in a letter dated January 31, 1927, to her cousin Harry A. Alexander; the letter also pokes fun at Isaiah Moses's piety:

"Once when he was Vice President of the Synagogue, he had indigestion, couldn't keep anything on his breadbasket, so the doctor told him to eat raw oysters – Great Mercy! What! Never! Against all Jewish law. No shell fish. Here our wonderful Grandma spoke up. She said, "take them as medicine, your health requires it to be done." Well in order not to set a wicked example to his family, he went out to the furthest corner of the Oaks with a trusted servant to open the oysters and began to eat the oysters – but alas! At that very corner just over the fence was a lot belonging to the Synagogue property. Just at that time two members came out to inspect it. What did they behold? Mr. Isaiah Moses, that pillar of the Synagogue, eating oysters!!! He was ordered to face the powers of the Congregation, but here again our Grandma came to the front. She brought the Doctor. He was absolved."

Rebecca was also active in Isaiah's business, probably from the beginning of her marriage, but especially after Isaiah bought the plantation. Her daybook lists accounts with family members over a period from 1846 to 1863, though the only known public listing of her as a businesswoman is the 1837 city directory that listed her as having a dry-goods business. In several pages of her daybook, photostatic copies of which are extant, she is shown to be a practical woman who kept detailed records on various transactions. A married woman could not generally do business legally on their own behalf unless granted the status of a sole trader by her husband. There is no evidence that Rebecca was ever made a sole trader as was a kinswoman, Ann Irby Huguenin Alexander, and her own daughter Hannah Moses Abrahams. As Isaiah's interests shifted from running his business to his plantation and then to intense involvement in the Esnoga, Rebecca undoubtedly played a larger role in running the business and may have run it herself for a number of years. It also appears from the dates of her daybook entries that she took over keeping track of transactions involving slaves once Isaiah had sold the plantation and probably lost interest in managing matters outside of congregational politics. Rebecca appears to have leased the services of slaves on an annual basis and commissioned her son Levy and son-in- law Adolph J. Brady to manage this business. In her daybook she lists the sale of a slave who had run away in Montgomery, Alabama, the town where Levy and his sons lived.

By the time of the Civil War, Rebecca's husband had died, and she was living with daughter Cecilia Moses Solomons and husband Abraham Alexander Solomons, a druggist originally licensed in S.C. but later a resident of Savannah.

A family story relates that in 1865, she heard a newsboy outside her bedroom window shouting the news that Lee had surrendered, and she had a stroke. Rebecca died in 1872, when she was 80 years old. She is buried next to Isaiah at the Coming Street Cemetery in Charleston.

More About Rebecca Phillips:
Residence: 1807, First recorded year in SC

More About Isaiah Moses:
Residence: 1811, First recorded year in SC
Role in KKBE Reforming: Between 1840 - 1843, Didn't sign petition to install an organ at KKBE.
Citation: **This Happy Land** by Hagy. Page 272

    v. Esther Phillips, born December 06, 1794; died January 23, 1883 in Augusta, GA; married Isaac Henricks.

Generation No. 10

750. Jacob Isaacks (Source: Malcolm H. Stern,

First American Jewish Familes - 600 Genealogies - 1654 - 1988, (Ottenheimer Publishers; 3rd ed. updated and rev edition (1988)), 120,190.), born 1718 in New York City, New York; died March 20, 1798 in Newport, RI. He was the son of **1500. Abraham Isaacks** and **1501. Hannah Mears**. He married **751. Rebecca Mears** October 08, 1760 in Newport, RI.

751. Rebecca Mears (Source: Malcolm H. Stern, *First American Jewish Familes - 600 Genealogies - 1654 - 1988*, (Ottenheimer Publishers; 3rd ed. updated and rev edition (1988)), 120,190.). She was the daughter of **1502. Judah Mears** and **1503. Jochabed Michaels**.

More About Jacob Isaacks and Rebecca Mears:
Marriage: October 08, 1760, Newport, RI

Children of Jacob Isaacks and Rebecca Mears are:

     i.   Abraham Isaacks (Source: (1) James William Hagy, *This Happy Land - The Jews of Colonial and Antebellium Charleston*, (The University of Alabama Press 1993), 333., (2) Malcolm H. Stern, *First American Jewish Familes - 600 Genealogies - 1654 - 1988*, (Ottenheimer Publishers; 3rd ed. updated and rev edition (1988)), 120.), died February 25, 1835 in Montgomery, Alabama; married Rebecca Cohen.

        More About Abraham Isaacks:
Residence: 1801, First recorded year in SC

ii. Grace Isaacks

iii. Josey Isaacks

iv. Judah Mears Isaacks (Source: (1)
James William Hagy, *This Happy
Land - The Jews of Colonial and
Antebellium Charleston*, (The
University of Alabama Press
1993), 334., (2) Malcolm H.
Stern, *First American Jewish
Families - 600 Genealogies - 1654 -
1988*, (Ottenheimer Publishers;
3rd ed. updated and rev edition
(1988)), 120.), died in
Charleston, South Carolina.

v. Rachel Isaacks (Source: (1)
James William Hagy, *This Happy
Land - The Jews of Colonial and
Antebellium Charleston*, (The
University of Alabama Press
1993), 334., (2) Malcolm H.
Stern, *First American Jewish
Families - 600 Genealogies - 1654 -
1988*, (Ottenheimer Publishers;
3rd ed. updated and rev edition
(1988)), 120.), born 1781; died
1803.

vi. Samson M. Isaacks, born June
13, 1783; died June 29, 1783.

vii. Jacob Isaacks, Jr., born 1785.

viii. Hannah Isaacks, died March 08,
1798; married Jacob Phillps
August 13, 1785 in Newport,
RI.

375

98

Generation No. 11

1500. Abraham Isaacks (Source: (1) Malcolm H.
Stern, *Americans of Jewish Descent: A Compendium of
Genealogy* , (Hebrew Union College Press, Cincinnati;
1st edition (1960)), 90., (2) Malcolm H. Stern, *First
American Jewish Families - 600 Genealogies - 1654 - 1988*,
(Ottenheimer Publishers; 3rd ed. updated and rev
edition (1988)), 120., (3) 1654 Society of Shearith
Israel Cemetery Project, Shearith Israel 21st Street
Cemetery NYC.), born 1658 in Emden, Friesland,
Holland (Later Ceded to Prussia); died September 24,
1743 in New York City, New York. He married **1501.
Hannah Mears**.

    1501. Hannah Mears (Source: Malcolm H.
Stern, *First American Jewish Families - 600 Genealogies -
1654 - 1988*, (Ottenheimer Publishers; 3rd ed.
updated and rev edition (1988)), 120.), died July 19,
1745 in New York, New York.

Notes for Abraham Isaacks:
Buried Cemetery of Cong. Shearith Israel, NYC. Near
the corner of 21st Street and 6th Ave
Stone reads:

"Here lies buried
The Venerable and honored married man Rabbi
Abraham son of Isaac (whose memory is a blessing)
From the city of Emden in Friesland
He died on the first of the middle days
of Tabernacles and was buried
The same Day in the year 5504 (1743) (24 September)
May his soul be bound up in the bond of life"

per Henry Aaron Alexander's book of 1954 on the Alexander Family (pages 69/70).

More About Abraham Isaacks:
Cemetery: September 24, 1743, Shearith Israel 21st Street Cemetery NYC
Emigration: 1697, Came to America
Freeman: August 06, 1723, Made a Freeman
Stone: 1697, Immigrated to the North America (NYC)

Children of Abraham Isaacks and Hannah Mears are:

   i. Michael Isaacks (Source: Malcolm H. Stern, *First American Jewish Families - 600 Genealogies - 1654 - 1988*, (Ottenheimer Publishers; 3rd ed. updated and rev edition (1988)), 120.).

   ii. Sarah Isaacks (Source: James William Hagy, *This Happy Land - The Jews of Colonial and Antebellium Charleston*, (The University of Alabama Press 1993), 334.).

750 iii. Jacob Isaacks, born 1718 in New York City, New York; died March 20, 1798 in Newport, RI; married Rebecca Mears October 08, 1760 in Newport, RI.

   iv. Judith Isaacks (Source: Malcolm H. Stern, *First American Jewish Families - 600 Genealogies - 1654 - 1988*, (Ottenheimer Publishers; 3rd ed. updated and rev edition

100

(1988)), 120.), born 1723.

v.   Riche Isaacks (Source: Malcolm H. Stern, *First American Jewish Families - 600 Genealogies - 1654 - 1988*, (Ottenheimer Publishers; 3rd ed. updated and rev edition (1988)), 120.), born 1733.

vi.   Moses Isaacks (Source: (1) Malcolm H. Stern, *First American Jewish Families - 600 Genealogies - 1654 - 1988*, (Ottenheimer Publishers; 3rd ed. updated and rev edition (1988)), 120., (2) Malcolm H. Stern, *Americans of Jewish Descent: A Compendium of Genealogy* , (Hebrew Union College Press, Cincinnati; 1st edition (1960)), 90.), born March 25, 1737; married Judith Rachel Mears August 30, 1764 in Philadelphia; born April 20, 1747 in New York; died June 06, 1818 in New York.

More About Moses Isaacks:
Residence: 1806, First recorded year in SC

More About Moses Isaacks and Judith Mears:
Marriage: August 30, 1764, Philadelphia

1502. Judah Mears (Source: (1) James William
Hagy, *This Happy Land - The Jews of Colonial and
Antebellium Charleston*, (The University of Alabama
Press 1993)., (2) Malcolm H. Stern, *First American
Jewish Families - 600 Genealogies - 1654 - 1988*,
(Ottenheimer Publishers; 3rd ed. updated and rev
edition (1988)), 190.), born in London, England; died
June 07, 1762 in Cape St. Francois, Guadeloupe. He
was the son of **3004. Sampson Mears** and **3005. Joy
Franks**. He married **1503. Jochabed Michaels**
1730.

1503. Jochabed Michaels (Source: (1) James
William Hagy, *This Happy Land - The Jews of Colonial
and Antebellium Charleston*, (The University of Alabama
Press 1993), 361., (2) Malcolm H. Stern, *First
American Jewish Families - 600 Genealogies - 1654 - 1988*,
(Ottenheimer Publishers; 3rd ed. updated and rev
edition (1988)), 190,193.). She was the daughter of
3006. Moses Michaels and **3007. Catharine H.
Machar**.

More About Judah Mears:
Emigration: 1728, Came to America from Cape St.
Francois, Guadeloupe
Freeman: May 30, 1738, Made Freeman

More About Judah Mears and Jochabed Michaels:
Marriage: 1730

Children of Judah Mears and Jochabed Michaels are:
     751   i.   Rebecca Mears, married Jacob
                       Isaacks October 08, 1760 in
                       Newport, RI.
           ii.   Judith Rachel Mears (Source: (1)
                       James William Hagy, *This Happy*

Land - The Jews of Colonial and Antebellium Charleston, (The University of Alabama Press 1993), 334., (2) Malcolm H. Stern, *First American Jewish Families - 600 Genealogies - 1654 - 1988*, (Ottenheimer Publishers; 3rd ed. updated and rev edition (1988)), 120,190., (3) Malcolm H. Stern, *Americans of Jewish Descent: A Compendium of Genealogy* , (Hebrew Union College Press, Cincinnati; 1st edition (1960)), 90.), born April 20, 1747 in New York; died June 06, 1818 in New York; married Moses Isaacks August 30, 1764 in Philadelphia; born March 25, 1737.

More About Moses Isaacks:
Residence: 1806, First recorded year in SC

More About Moses Isaacks and Judith Mears:
Marriage: August 30, 1764, Philadelphia

Generation No. 12

3004. Sampson Mears (Source: (1) Malcolm H. Stern, *First American Jewish Families - 600 Genealogies - 1654 - 1988*, (Ottenheimer Publishers; 3rd ed.

updated and rev edition (1988)), 190., (2) Malcolm H. Stern, *Americans of Jewish Descent: A Compendium of Genealogy* , (Hebrew Union College Press, Cincinnati; 1st edition (1960)), 134.), born 1670 in London, England; died 1711 in London, England. He married **3005. Joy Franks**.

3005. Joy Franks (Source: Malcolm H. Stern, *First American Jewish Families - 600 Genealogies - 1654 - 1988*, (Ottenheimer Publishers; 3rd ed. updated and rev edition (1988)), 190.).

Children of Sampson Mears and Joy Franks are:

1502	i.	Judah Mears, born in London, England; died June 07, 1762 in Cape St. Francois, Guadeloupe; married Jochabed Michaels 1730.
	ii.	Grace Mears

3006. Moses Michaels, born August 08, 1677 in Herzfeld, Germany; died 1740 in Curacoa. He married **3007. Catharine H. Machar**.

3007. Catharine H. Machar

Children of Moses Michaels and Catharine Machar are:

1503	i.	Jochabed Michaels, married Judah Mears 1730.
	ii.	Rebecca Michael, married Judah Hays.
	iii.	Rachel Michael, died August 20, 1749 in New York, New York; married (1) Samuel Myers-Cohen; married (2) Jacob Levy

1744.

iv.   Blume Michael, married Aaron Louzada.

v.   Michael Michael, died March 1737 in New York, New York.

Bibliography of Sources

1654 Society of Shearith Israel Cemetery Project, Shearith Israel 21st Street Cemetery NYC.
> Medium: Tombstone. Location: internet.

Barnett Elzas, *The Jews of South Carolina, from the Earliest Times to the Present Day* , (Copyright 1905. First Edition).
> Medium: Book. Location: Larry Freudenberg Archives.

Barnett Elzas, *The Old Jewish Cemeteries at Charleston, SC*, (The Daggett Printing Company 1903).
> Medium: Book. Location: Larry Freudenberg Archives.
> Comments: A Transcript of the Inscriptions on their Tombstones. 1762 - 1903.

"Charleston News & Courier."
> Medium: Newspaper. Comments: The News & Courier. January 5, 1878.

Coming Street Cemetery.
> Medium: Tombstone. Location: Charleston, SC.
> Comments: The Coming Street Cemetery, established in 1762, is the oldest Jewish burial ground in the South. Privately owned by Kahal Kadosh Beth Elohim Synagogue, the cemetery contains some 600 marble and brownstone grave markers. Most of the markers date to the last half of the 18th century or the first half of the 19th century, and include box tombs, table-top tombs, obelisks, and columns. Many are significant examples of gravestone art, signed by locally prominent sculptors and stonecutters.

Confederate Veteren.
> Medium: Other.

Eugene W. Jones Jr., *Enlisted for the War - The Struggles of the Gallant 24th Regiment, SC Volunteers, Infantry 1861-1865*, (Longstreet House 1997).
> Medium: Book. Call number: 0944413439. Location: Larry Freudenberg Archives.

Henry Aaron Alexander, *Notes on The Alexander Family of South Carolina and Georgia and Connections - 1651-1954*, (1954).
> Medium: Book. Location: Larry Freudenberg Archives.

J. C. Garlington, *Men of the Time: Sketches of Living Notables. A*

Biographical Encyclopedia of Contemporaneous SC Leaders,
(Published 1902, Garlington Publishing, Spartenburg, SC).

> Medium: Book. Location: Original from the New York
> Public Library. Quality: Digitized by Google.

James William Hagy, *This Happy Land - The Jews of Colonial
and Antebellium Charleston*, (The University of Alabama Press
1993).

> Medium: Book. Call number: 0817312889. Location:
> Larry Freudenberg Archives.

Judith Shanks, Rebeccas Isiah Moses by Rebecca's great-,
great-, great-granddaughter.

> Medium: Internet.

KKBE Hugenin Avenue Cemetery.

> Medium: Tombstone. Location: Charleston, SC.
> Comments: Photos of stones taken by Larry
> Freudenberg.

Larry W. Freudenberg, Interview with Adelaide Jacobs nee
Triest, 1990's in Charleston.

> Medium: Interview. Location: Charleston. Comments:
> Interviews and conversations with great aunt Adelaide
> Triest Jacobs.

Larry W. Freudenberg, Rodeph Sholom Cemetery Rome,
GA.

> Medium: Tombstone. Comments: Photos of the
> stones during a visit to the cemetery in 1990.

Larry W. Freudenberg, Interview with Caroline Louise
Triest, 1990's in Charleston.

> Medium: Interview. Location: Charleston. Comments:
> Private interviews and conversations with my great
> Aunt Caroline Louise Triest. .

Larry W. Freudenberg, Interview with Margot Freudenberg
nee Strauss, 1990's in Charleston.

> Medium: Interview. Location: Charleston.

Magnolia Cemetery.

> Medium: Tombstone. Location: 702 Third Street
> Augusta, GA. Comments: Visit to cemetery and
> photos taken of stones. The land where Magnolia
> Cemetery is located was at one time part of a
> plantation with the first official burial in August of
> 1818. Academy of Richmond County owned the first
> two blocks and they sold it to the City Council of
> Augusta for $800.00 in 1817. Monies donated by

Mrs. Louise de L'Aigle Reese built the present office building in the memory of her mother, Mrs. Mary Clarke de L'Aigle. The cemetery contains over 60 acres. In the cemetery, you will find five (5) Jewish cemeteries and one (1) Greek cemetery. There is also a Masonic Lodge section and several church sections located in this one cemetery. .

Malcolm H. Stern, *First American Jewish Familes - 600 Genealogies - 1654 - 1988*, (Ottenheimer Publishers; 3rd ed. updated and rev edition (1988)).

> Medium: Book. Call number: B0007CBP0A. Location: American Jewish Archives Online.

Malcolm H. Stern, *Americans of Jewish Descent: A Compendium of Genealogy* , (Hebrew Union College Press, Cincinnati; 1st edition (1960)).

> Medium: Book. Call number: 87068-168-0. Location: Larry Freudenberg Archives. Comments: Library of Congress Catalogue Card Number: 60-14010.

Mourning Book of Heynemann Freudenberg, (Includes newspaper articles, obituaries, condolance letters).

> Medium: Book. Location: Larry Freudenberg Archives.

Revolutionary War Veteren.

Robert N. Rosen, *The Jewish Confederates*, (University of SC Press 2000).

> Medium: Book. Call number: 1570033633. Location: Larry Freudenberg Archives.

Submitted by Dorothy Ida Morse nee Levy, *Application for Membership to The National Society of the Daughters of the American Revolution*, (Application approved January 31, 1928).

> Medium: Official Document. Call number: 238769. Location: DAR records. Comments: Dorothy applied for membership as a Decendant of Jacob Phillips, her 3rd Great Grandfather.

Theodore and Dale Rosengarten, *A Portion of the People - Three Hundred Years of Southern Jewish Life*, (University of SC Press 2000).

> Medium: Book. Call number: 1570034451. Location: Larry Freudenberg Archives.

Thomas J. Tobias, *Tombstones That Tell Stories*, (Revised by Solomon Breibart 2000).

> Medium: Book. Location: Larry Freudenberg Archives.

USA, *Census.*
> Medium: Census.

Walter Freudenberg, *WWI Scrapbooks of Walter Freudenberg,* (Photos from WWI where Walter was an officer in the German army), "fig."
> Medium: Photograph. Location: Larry Freudenberg
> Archives.

War of 1812 Veteren.